REAGAN AT BERGEN-BELSEN AND BITBURG

D1526349

Library of Presidential Rhetoric

Martin J. Medhurst, General Editor

Reagan at Bergen-Belsen and Bitburg

Richard J. Jensen

Texas A&M University Press : College Station

This paper meets the requirements
of ANSI/NISO Z39.48-1992
(Permanence of Paper).
Binding materials chosen for durability.

Frontispiece: Ronald Reagan and Gen. Matthew Ridgway
at Bitburg Cemetery on May 5, 1985.
Photo courtesy the Ronald Reagan Presidential Library.

Library of Congress Cataloging-in-Publication Data

Jensen, Richard J. (Richard Jay), 1943–

Reagan at Bergen-Belsen and Bitburg / Richard J. Jensen. — 1st ed.

p. cm. — (Library of presidential rhetoric)

Includes bibliographical references and index.

ISBN-13: 978-1-58544-623-0 (cloth : alk. paper)

ISBN-10: 1-58544-623-8 (cloth : alk. paper)

ISBN-13: 978-1-58544-625-4 (pbk. : alk. paper)

ISBN-10: 1-58544-625-4 (paper : alk. paper)

1. Reagan, Ronald—Oratory.   2. Reagan, Ronald—Travel—Germany—Bergen Belsen—
Public opinion.   3. Reagan, Ronald—Travel—Germany—Bitburg—Public opinion.
4. Rhetoric—Political aspects—United States—History—20th century.
5. Communication in politics—United States—History—20th century.   6. Presidents—
United States—Language—History—20th century.   7. Political oratory—United States.
8. Discourse analysis—United States.   I. Title.

E877.2.J46   2007

973.927092—dc22   2007012894

Contents

Preface

The task of writing a book on Ronald Reagan is a daunting one because so much has been published about Reagan's life and career in books, scholarly journals, and the popular press. Any author who undertakes a study of Reagan finds it difficult to provide new information or insights about the life and actions of this controversial individual.

Writings about Reagan fall roughly into two groupings: those that strongly supported him and those that adamantly opposed him and his policies. It is virtually impossible to find anyone whose views of Ronald Reagan were neutral. When I mentioned to people that I was writing a book on Reagan and his rhetoric, their reactions fell into two opposing groupings: those who were interested in knowing more about Reagan and his speeches and those who did not really think he was worthy of such a study because he was greatly overrated as an orator and as a president.

This book focuses on Reagan as a presidential orator. Because of his unique ability to speak in public, Reagan was often called "The Great Communicator." Although no one seems to have identified the source of that label, it has been accepted in the popular press and in books and scholarly studies about Reagan and has become part of his persona and legacy. All the same, several people have made it clear to me that they do not consider Reagan a great communicator and have always been mystified by his success and the label.

Many authors have tried to describe what made Reagan a successful presidential orator. This book builds on the ideas of those previous writers and I hope adds insights about Reagan as a presidential speaker. It can easily be said that Reagan was a rhetorical animal, one whose career was based on his ability as a public speaker, whether representing the film industry and major corporations or in the political arena. Richard Reeves summarizes Reagan's dependence on speaking by claiming that Reagan "knew one very big thing about leadership and leaders: Words are usually more important than deeds."[1] In this study I attempt to illustrate Reagan's emphasis on words by analyzing two ceremonial speeches he delivered in West Germany on May 5, 1985: one at the site of the Bergen-Belsen concentration camp and another later in the day at the U.S. Air Force base in Bitburg. Immediately preceding the Bitburg speech, Reagan made a highly controversial visit to a German military cemetery near the base.

When the editor of the Library of Presidential Rhetoric asked me to undertake this study, he proposed that I focus my analysis on the speech Reagan delivered at Bitburg. As I studied the events leading to the Bitburg speech, it became clear that the speech delivered earlier in the day at the site of the Bergen-Belsen concentration camp was intimately linked with the Bitburg speech, had a definite effect on the message Reagan delivered at Bitburg, and affected the perception of the Bitburg speech in the eyes of the press and many members of the public. Some observers argued that the speech at Bergen-Belsen was more significant, meaningful, and successful than the one at Bitburg. I decided that it would make sense to evaluate both speeches.

As becomes clear, the speeches in West Germany were delivered in an atmosphere of great controversy, but Reagan ignored much of the criticism and his speeches contained many ideas his critics would find unacceptable. The speeches were written by two of Reagan's best speechwriters, with input from Reagan and other members of his staff. They were carefully organized and well written, but it was probably not possible for Reagan to defuse totally the criticism offered by his opponents. His supporters would argue, however, that the speeches were successful because they met the expectation of the audience and occasion and reduced the level of criticism from Reagan's opponents. Critics see Reagan's reactions to the controversy and his failure to defuse the criticism of his actions and words as the first major failure of his second term as president.

In this book I outline the events leading to the speeches and the controversy surrounding the president's trip to West Germany, discuss Reagan's abilities as an orator, outline the preparation for the speeches, analyze the speeches, and evaluate their degree of success or failure. I also compare two highly successful ceremonial speeches celebrating the fortieth anniversary of D-Day on June 6, 1984, to the speeches at Bergen-Belsen and Bitburg. The D-Day speeches illustrate that Reagan and his staff were capable of creating effective ceremonial speeches outside the United States. This is a formidable undertaking for such a brief book, and many of the ideas presented here are more suggestive than conclusive.

I had the great fortune of teaching courses in public address for three decades at the university level. In those years I often asked students to analyze Reagan's speeches in my classes. It was clear that students could learn a great deal by watching a video of Reagan or by analyzing the written texts of his speeches. Reagan was an intriguing model for students learning to prepare and deliver speeches. Although they often did not agree with Reagan's ideas or his politics, my students seemed to learn a great deal about rhetoric from his public speeches. This book incorporates many of the ideas I used in the classroom in an attempt to understand Reagan's success as a speaker. Many of the techniques Reagan adopted could be used by anyone interested in learning how to speak effectively or improving his or her rhetorical skills. In some respects, then, this volume can be seen as a kind of handbook on how to create and deliver a ceremonial speech to the public.

I would like to express my appreciation to Shelly Jacobs and Ben Pezzillo for their invaluable help during my research at the Ronald Reagan Presidential Library in Simi Valley, California. Josh Gilder provided valuable insights into the preparation and writing of the Bitburg speech. I thank Martin J. Medhurst, the editor of this series, for giving me the opportunity to undertake this study of Reagan. In the process, I have learned a great deal about Reagan and about politics in general. I also express my appreciation to the staff at Texas A&M University Press in general and Mary Lenn Dixon in particular for their excellent work in publishing this book and two previous books on Cesar Chavez.

I also wish to express my appreciation to my good friends Ron and Grace Bousek for their encouragement through the preparation of this book. A final thanks goes to my family: my wife Carol Jensen, my daughter Mary Kay Holmes, my son-in-law Brian Holmes, and my beautiful granddaughters, Hazel Holmes and Sadie Holmes.

Ronald Reagan's Remarks at a Commemorative Ceremony at Bergen-Belsen Concentration Camp in the Federal Republic of Germany

May 5, 1985

Chancellor Kohl and honored guests, this painful walk into the past has done much more than remind us of the war that consumed the European Continent. What we have seen makes unforgettably clear that no one of the rest of us can fully understand the enormity of the feelings carried by the victims of these camps. The survivors carry a memory beyond anything that we can comprehend. The awful evil started by one man, an evil that victimized all of the world with its destruction, was uniquely destructive of the millions forced into the grim abyss of these camps.

Here lie people—Jews—whose death was inflicted for no other reason than their very existence. Their pain was borne only because of who they were and because of the God in their prayers. Alongside them lay many Christians—Catholics and Protestants.

For year after year, until that man and his evil were destroyed, hell yawned forth its awful contents. People were brought here for no other purpose but to suffer and die—to go unfed when hungry, uncared for when sick, tortured when the whim struck, and left to have misery consume them when all there was around them was misery.

I'm sure we all share similar first thoughts, and that is: What of the youngsters who died at this dark stalag? All was gone for them forever—not to feel again the warmth of life's sunshine and promise, not the laughter and splendid ache of growing up, nor the consoling embrace of a family. Try to think of being young and never having a day without searing emotional and physical pain—desolate, unrelieved pain.

Today, we've been grimly reminded why the commandant of this camp was named "the Beast of Belsen." Above all, we're struck by the horror of it all—the monstrous, incomprehensible horror. And that's what we've seen but is what we can never understand as the victims did. Nor with all our compassion can we feel what the survivors feel to this day and what they will feel as long as they live. What we've felt and are expressing with words cannot convey the suffering that they endured. That is why history will forever brand what happened as the Holocaust.

Here, death ruled, but we've learned something as well. Because of what happened, we found that death cannot rule forever, and that's why we're here today. We're here because humanity refuses to accept that freedom of the spirit of man can ever be extinguished. We're here to commemorate that life triumphed over the tragedy and death of the Holocaust—overcame the suffering, the sickness, the testing and, yes, the gassings. We're here today to confirm that the horror cannot outlast hope, and that even from the worst of all things, the best may come forth. Therefore, even out of this overwhelming sadness, there must be some purpose, and there is. It comes to us through the transforming love of God.

We learn from the Talmud that: "It was only through suffering that the children of Israel obtained three priceless and coveted gifts: The Torah, the land of Israel, and the World to Come." Yes, out of this sickness—as crushing and cruel as it was—there was hope for the world as well as for the world to come. Out of the ashes—hope, and from all the pain—promise.

So much of this is symbolized today by the fact that most of the leadership of free Germany is represented here today. Chancellor Kohl, you and your countrymen have made real the renewal that had to happen. Your nation and the German people have been strong and resolute in your willingness to confront and condemn the acts of a hated regime of the past. This reflects the courage of your people and your devotion to freedom and justice since the war. Think how far we've come from that time when despair made these tragic victims wonder if anything could survive.

As we flew here from Hanover, low over the greening farms and the emerging springtime of the lovely German countryside, I reflected, and there must have been a time when the prisoners at Bergen-Belsen and those of every other camp must have felt the springtime was gone forever from their lives. Surely we can understand that when we see what is around us—all these children of God under bleak and lifeless mounds, the plainness of which does not even hint at the unspeakable acts that created them. Here they lie, never to hope, never to pray, never to love, never to heal, never to laugh, never to cry.

And too many of them knew that this was their fate, but that was not the end. Through it all was their faith and a spirit that moved their faith.

Nothing illustrates this better than the story of a young girl who died here Bergen-Belsen. For more than 2 years Anne Frank and her family had hidden from the Nazis in a confined annex in Holland where she kept a remarkably profound diary. Betrayed by an informant, Anne and her family were sent by freight car first to Auschwitz and finally here to Bergen-Belsen.

Just 3 weeks before her capture, young Anne wrote these words: "It's really a wonder that I haven't dropped all my ideals because they seem so absurd and impossible to carry out. Yet I keep them because in spite of everything I still believe that people are good at heart. I simply can't build up my hopes on a foundation consisting of confusion, misery, and death. I see the world gradually being turned into a wilderness. I hear the ever approaching thunder which will destroy us too; I can feel the suffering of millions and yet, if I looked up into the heavens I think that it will all come right, that this cruelty too will end and that peace and tranquility will return again." Eight months later, this sparkling young life ended here at Bergen-Belsen. Somewhere here lies Anne Frank.

Everywhere here are memories—pulling us, touching us, making us understand that they can never be erased. Such memories take us where God intended his children to go—toward learning, toward healing, and, above all, toward redemption. They beckon us through the endless stretches of our heart to the knowing commitment that the life of each individual can change the world and make it better.

We're all witnesses; we share the glistening hope that rests in every human soul. Hope leads us, if we're prepared to trust it, toward what out President Lincoln called the better angels of our nature. And then, rising above all this cruelty, out of this tragic and nightmarish time, beyond the anguish, the pain and the suffering for all time, we can and must pledge: Never again.

CHAPTER 1

Ronald Reagan: A Maddeningly Contradictory Figure

When Ronald Reagan died on June 5, 2004, there was an outpouring of writing about his accomplishments as president and descriptions of the personal traits that made his election as president of the United States possible. Many writings expressed a similar theme: the difficulty of truly understanding this complex individual. As one article states, "The passing of the fortieth president marks the close of one of the great American sagas: the rise and reign of the mysterious and elusive Ronald Reagan. . . . In the White House, Reagan proved a maddeningly contradictory figure."[1]

In this chapter I detail some of the contradictions in Reagan's personality, outline the reactions to Reagan by his followers and critics, provide a brief overview of his life and speaking career, introduce some of the reasons for his effectiveness as a speaker, and begin a discussion of his ceremonial speeches at events commemorating the end of World War II. The information in this chapter is useful for understanding Reagan's public statements and actions during his controversial trip to West Germany in 1985 as well as the prominent role speaking played in his presidency.

Reagan's Contradictions

Reagan proved to be a mystery even to those who studied him over an extended period. Lou Cannon, Reagan's most prominent biographer, describes the Reagan paradox: "On one level he seemed the 'citizen-politician' he claimed to be, almost completely ignorant of even civics-book information about how bills were passed or how an administration functioned. But on another level, he seemed the most consummate and effective politician I had ever met."[2]

Cannon summarizes how this mysterious individual was viewed by observers in and out of government: "In the presidency . . . Reagan seemed such a simple straightforward man that it was often said of him that 'what you saw was what you got.' After he had been president for a while, however, the prevailing view in Washington became that what the people most often saw was the work of his staff, his cabinet, his political advisors, or his wife. This low opinion of Reagan deprived him of credit for some of his accomplishments but also spared him the blame for his shortcomings. And it helped Reagan remain an elusive figure, for all his popularity."[3]

Although observers may not have understood Reagan, his followers loved him as an individual and greatly admired his achievements as president. Rhetorical scholar William F. Lewis captures the myth that Reagan's supporters accepted and proclaimed about his election to the presidency: "By 1980, America had lost its sense of direction. Economic troubles, a series of foreign policy failures, and corruption had created a national malaise. Then Ronald Reagan came onto the scene with a vision of America that reinvigorated the nation. His great skills as a communicator and his commitment to fundamental ideals were just what the nation needed. We were once again proud to be Americans."[4] Peggy Noonan, a Reagan speechwriter, provides an additional element to the Reagan myth: "Through the force of his beliefs and with a deep natural dignity he restored a great and fallen office."[5]

Communication scholar Sarah Russell Hankins proposes that Reagan played the role of an American hero. That role allowed him and his followers to create "mythic characterizations" of the president before and after his election. Hankins argues that Reagan became "the classic hero of the Old West" who saved the United States in the eyes of his admirers.[6] Reagan often portrayed a cowboy during his acting career and built on that image during his years in political office, so it would be easy to describe him in the terms of the Western hero, a kind of American hero that many members of the public would find particularly attractive.

Lewis agrees that Reagan was revered as a hero, but he proposes that Reagan played that role in a unique way: "This familiar and well accepted story follows the pattern of many political success stories in which the hero rescues the country from a time of great trouble. This story is special, however, in that Reagan is said to have accomplished the feat through the power of speaking." Lewis writes that Reagan was often referred to as "the Western world's most gifted communicator."[7]

Not only did Reagan's followers believe myths about him, but Reagan himself lived in a world populated with myths: "Reagan somehow operated on a different plane from most politicians; he moved in a world of myths and symbols, not facts and programs."[8] Reagan deeply believed in myths about the United States and used them in his public discourse, "so he was extraordinarily good at inspiring the rest of the country to similarly suspend belief. . . . Part of Reagan's success as a leader lay in the fact that most of the myths he created were preferable to reality."[9] As columnist Richard Reeves writes, "Reagan was not a man of vision, he was a man of imagination—and he believed in the past he imagined."[10]

Reagan's Critics

Although supporters claimed that Reagan reenergized the country and the presidency after years of weak, ineffective presidents, he had a host of critics who argued that he was also an ineffective president. Columnist Thomas L. Friedman summarizes their view when he states that Reagan was "the most overrated president in U.S. history."[11] Lewis claims that there were so many writings that expressed disagreement with Reagan that they created a genre, a unique type or kind of message whose commonality was based on their opposition to Reagan and his policies.[12]

Many negative analyses questioned Reagan's abilities as a leader by labeling him "uninformed, irrational, and inconsistent."[13] Critics described Reagan as a disinterested, aloof administrator who relied on his staff to do most of his work: "As Reagan saw it—and those around him did nothing to dissuade him of the notion—a President was like the chairman of the board of a large corporation and his Cabinet was his board of directors. That had been his approach to state government and, as he made clear throughout those months before he took office, that was how he intended to run Washington."[14] Mayer and McManus summarize one of the major weaknesses of that kind of leadership: "In Reagan's permissive White House, policy making was literally up for grabs; proximity to the president was tantamount to power itself."[15]

Critics also argued that Reagan had a "striking lack of interest in international issues. Unlike every president in modern times, he showed little passion for the details of foreign policy."[16] Because he did not have passion for or interest in foreign affairs, Reagan was not well informed about many important issues. This lack of interest may be a partial explanation for his lack of confidence in his ability to speak success-fully during international trips. If Reagan did not understand people in foreign countries or the issues that concerned those audiences, he would have a difficult time reaching out to them in his presidential addresses.

Unfortunately for Reagan's critics, Lewis proposes, "journalistic and scholarly analysis debunking his competence and sincerity was largely irrelevant through most of his presidency."[17] Many people in the United States were unaware of Reagan's limitations as a leader and not concerned that information in his messages was often incomplete or inaccurate. They were so positively inspired by Reagan's public persona and speaking that his shortcomings were not relevant or even important. As Mayer and McManus state, "Reagan was larger than life. . . . voters had an extraordinary affection for him."[18] Many of them continue to have extraordinary affection today.

Reagan's Supporters

Although many writings painted a negative picture of Reagan, others composed an opposing genre built on the myth of Reagan as a dynamic, creative leader with extraordinary abilities as a communicator. Much of the public debate during the Reagan presidency could be seen as a battle between those who trusted and admired him and those who had serious doubts about his abilities and intellect. Both groups admitted, however, that he used the spoken word successfully in a manner that few presidents in history had achieved.

After Reagan left office, many of his strongest supporters wrote books and articles that helped extend his image as a mythical leader.[19] There are even those who saw Reagan and his administration as providing lessons that could be used as guidelines for one's daily life.[20]

Economist Martin Anderson, a former Reagan aide, provides a typical positive description of Reagan and the pivotal role he played in creating his own legacy: "He did not create the intellectual-political revolution that swept the world in the 1980s but he was its political leader, its driving force. He led the United States back to greatness—in the power of its military defenses, the strength of its economy—the freedom of its people—and by doing so established our country as a towering model of a good society. In a world dark with cruel oppression, desperate poverty, and crushed human spirits, the United States rose ever higher as a brilliant, powerful beacon of justice and peace and prosperity."[21]

Anderson argues that Reagan was misunderstood by his opponents and that "even some of his closest political colleagues in the White House and the cabinet seemed to fail to appreciate that behind the warm geniality lay a calculating, imaginative mind governed by a steely will."[22] He paints a picture of an intelligent, well-informed individual: "He is highly intelligent, with a photographic memory. He has a gift for absorbing great amounts of diverse information, and is capable of combining various parts of that information into new, coherent packages, and then conveying his thought and ideas clearly and concisely in a way that is understandable to almost anyone."[23] Josh Gilder, a Reagan speechwriter, saw him as a disciplined individual who did a tremendous amount of work each evening after he left the office—contrary to the image that Reagan did little work either in the Oval Office or in his private quarters.[24]

But Anderson may be inadvertently supporting some of Reagan's opponents' beliefs when he describes Reagan's management style: "So everyone overlooked and compensated for the fact that he made decisions like an ancient king or a Turkish pasha, passively letting his subjects serve him, selecting only those morsels of public policy that were especially tasty. Rarely did he ask searching questions and demand to know why someone had or had not done something. He just sat back in a supremely calm, relaxed manner and waited until important things were brought to him. And then he would act, quickly, decisively, and usually, very wisely."[25]

Understanding Ronald Reagan

Perhaps no one understood Reagan better than Lou Cannon. Cannon describes what he believes was Reagan's essence as a leader and communicator: "The greatness of Reagan was not that he was in America, but that America was inside of him."[26] Reagan had a knack for understanding and then expressing ideas that were important to a majority of Americans. Michael Deaver, a member of Reagan's staff in California and the White House, explains Reagan's relationship to the public this way: "The Reagan Revolution succeeded, not because the president told the people what they wanted to hear. He told them what *he* wanted to hear—and for most of America it was the same thing."[27]

Deaver points to another important aspect in understanding Reagan and his success as a politician: "The key to understanding Ronald Reagan is to know that he has been underestimated all his life."[28] Because people did not take Reagan seriously, he was able to defeat opponents who either seemed stronger or felt that they were superior to him. This underestimation occurred when Reagan first ran for governor of California and continued through his years in the White House.

Deaver also proposes that anyone who wished to understand Reagan should observe how he focused on a set of core beliefs and goals and ignored information that challenged them: "As much as anyone I have known, Reagan attaches himself to a cause rather than people."[29] Those causes and beliefs were consistent throughout Reagan's career and gave him a strong foundation for his ideas and his messages.

Cannon describes another trait critical to an understanding of Reagan and his actions. Cannon's observation is particularly crucial for this study because it helps us understand Reagan's reactions to the controversy surrounding his trip to Germany: "When he changed positions on an issue and even when he changed political parties, he insisted that he was being consistent with his past record and that it was others who had changed. He was slow to anger but extremely stubborn. He detested arguments. He trusted everyone who worked with him and considered even mild criticism of the most incompetent subordinate to be a disguised attack on him or his policy. . . . He thought of himself as a man of principle, and he was difficult to push on the issues that mattered most to him. As President he was the most malleable and least movable of men."[30]

Reagan as Presidential Orator

Although he was a complex individual, for many the essence of Ronald Reagan could be found in his ability to speak effectively to the American public. As newscaster Dan Rather states: "Many have called President Reagan the Great Communicator, and the label sometimes grates on his partisans, who see in it a reluctance to credit the Reagan ideology. But to Reagan detractors and defenders alike, one might ask: Just what is leadership, in a democracy, but the harnessing of policy to the horse of persuasion? In a successful presidency, these realms are inseparable, and this was something that President Reagan always seemed to grasp. . . . To recall President Reagan's speeches . . . is to remember a time not so long ago when words still reached out to the American imagination."[31]

Deaver echoes Rather's words: "I did not create the label The Great

Communicator. I don't know who did. I only know that he ranks with FDR and John Kennedy, in this century, as presidents who could deliver a speech with the power to move people. He is, after all, a performer."[32] Although no one seemed to know who created the label, it was adopted by many in the media and in the general public and has continued as part of the Reagan legacy.

Although he was called "The Great Communicator," Reagan claimed that his success was not based on his speaking skills but on the subjects of his speeches: "I wasn't a great communicator, but I communicated great things, and they didn't spring full bloom from my brow, they came from the head of a great nation—from our experience, our wisdom, and . . . the principles that have guided us for two centuries."[33] Reagan repeated many of the same themes throughout his years as an actor and a politician: "That's one of my theories about political speechmaking. You have to keep pounding away with your message, year after year because that's the only way it will sink into the collective consciousness."[34] Those who followed Reagan's career referred to his standard message as the "The Speech," because he gave essentially the same speech thousands of times in his career as a spokesperson for the film industry, as a consultant for General Electric, and as a politician.[35] Deaver writes that "Reagan took The Speech to any crowd that would have him. It was the beginning of the 'common sense' agenda that he would talk about incessantly, and with ever-greater effect, for more than three decades."[36]

Although Reagan claimed that ideas were the reason for his success, he worked hard to develop his speaking techniques and continued to refine them throughout his career. As Deaver writes, "He must have given the same campaign speech ten thousand times, but he practiced it in its entirety before each session. He would not be caught flatfooted."[37] Josh Gilder, the author of the Bitburg speech, says that Reagan practiced every speech before he delivered it, that he worked constantly at his speeches throughout this presidency.[38]

Reagan was fortunate to have a voice that aided his success as a speaker. As Deaver states, "The words he did say and the way he said them were often memorable. Reagan clearly knew that his soft, inviting tenor was his bread and butter, in large part responsible for Reagan's success in politics, business, and film. Most great orators of our time wave their arms or gesture majestically with their hands. Clenched fists fly in the air, and fingers point like piercing daggers—but never Reagan. He didn't need his body for emphasis. The pure resonance of that voice was enough."[39]

In addition to possessing natural talents as a speaker and working to refine those talents, Reagan learned that it was crucial to create strong connections between himself and his audience. Deaver notes Reagan's insistence on that connection: "He wanted the audience to have the same amount of ownership in the event as he did. It was a marriage in his view, not an address, and like any partnership, it required a mutual commitment. He liked to see into their eyes, to gauge the effectiveness of his words and movements. Every speech was a new adventure, not just as paid company man or governor, but as president as well. He would be the first to admit it." Reagan developed a method that worked for him: "Reagan also learned before entering politics that to connect with your crowd, you need to be physically close to them. Since the lights were already on, per his direction, he wanted to be sure that his listeners were within striking distance. I was to instruct the organizers to put the first row no more than eight feet from the lectern. If the front row were any farther back, I'd hear about it later. He wanted eye contact."[40]

Rhetorical critics Kurt Ritter and David Henry write that Reagan was able to connect with his audience by assuming "the demeanor of a comforting pastor to the country." That character allowed him to add dignity to his messages: "Reagan's oratorical success owes as much to his capacity to imbue secular political events and issues with the trappings of religious ritual as it does to undeniably appealing delivery skills." The "most salient features" of Reagan's rhetoric include "unself-conscious references to God, emphasis on heroes, appeals to values of freedom and progress, and Reagan's fitting presentational manner."[41] Reagan himself admitted that he assumed the role of a pastor: "I became a kind of preacher. I'd preach in my speeches about the problems we had and try to get people aroused and to say to their neighbors, 'Hey, let's do something about this.'"[42]

Much of Reagan's success as a secular pastor, politician, and leader was based on a warm personality that made people feel comfortable when they were near him or heard him speak. Even one of his harshest critics, historian Garry Wills, describes Reagan as an extremely charming man who was able to unite many segments of the American public "around his radiant personality." He elaborates: "He comforted the comfortable and disarmed the afflicted. He was too obviously nice to mean whatever meanness appeared in his programs. He gave conservatism the elements it had signally lacked—humanity, optimism, hope.... Reagan, without much wit or passion or intelligence, had a humanity that made up for anything he lacked. He was the first truly cheerful conservative, and America is a country that does not recognize itself unless it sees, in the mirror, a confident face looking back at it."[43]

Noonan, like many of his supporters, was charmed by Reagan's personality: "He was probably the sweetest, most innocent man ever to serve in the Oval Office. He was a modest man with an intellect slightly superior to the average. His whole career, in fact, was proof of the superior power of goodness to gifts. 'No great men are good men,' said Lord Acton, who was right, until Reagan."[44]

Reagan's Presidential Leadership

David Gergen, a White House advisor in several administrations and a student of presidential leadership, observes that Reagan was a natural to politics, like many "who seemed blessed with instincts and intuitions that set them apart as leaders." He continues by saying that "Reagan had a magic that came easily and made others seem plodding." But Reagan had a major flaw in that he "could be so dreamy and inattentive to detail that he allowed dramatic mistakes to occur. He had less curiosity about public policy than any president since perhaps the 1920s."[45]

Reagan often was not involved in the day-to-day operations of the White House. According to Cannon, "He could act decisively when presented with clear options, but he rarely initiated a meeting, a phone call, a proposal, or an idea. He thought his staff would tell him anything he ought to know and invested most of his energy and interest in the public performances of the presidency."[46] Even an admirer like Peter Robinson, one of Reagan's speechwriters, points out that Reagan did not take the lead in many of the administration's actions: "Reagan . . . concentrated his attention on the few tasks he alone could perform. He set overall administration policies, made two or three critical decisions a day, and gave speeches in which he explained his goals to the American people. He left everything else to the staff. That gave him plenty of time to exercise, get his sleep, and enjoy himself, activities that in turn enabled him to remain fresh and composed in performing his duties as President."[47]

Reagan's biographers note that his lack of oversight led to constant internal battle among his staff: "There are always power struggles in a Reagan administration, precisely because he dislikes them so much. He averts his eyes from the first signs of them. He cannot control them because he cannot bring himself to look at them."[48]

Even though he may not have been actively involved in the day-to-day functioning of his office, Reagan gave the appearance of being in charge. Mayer and McManus argue that Reagan "mastered the ceremonial and symbolic functions of the office so that he could act presidential even when he wasn't, in the traditional sense, functioning like one."[49] Because people saw Reagan acting like a strong leader, they believed that he was in control of his office and his staff, but much of that control was only in appearance.

During his years as governor of California and his first term in the White House, Reagan had a highly efficient staff that included many of the same loyal, dedicated individuals. During his second term, however, many of these people left government or moved from the White House to jobs in other government departments and agencies. As a result, Reagan faced his second term with a less effective and loyal staff. As presidential advisor Ed Rollins says, "All his life, Ronald Reagan has been lucky to be protected by people who had his best interests at heart. . . . That changed."[50]

Reagan rejected the criticism that he was a "hands-off" manager and claimed that such attacks were made by people who did not understand how he operated. In his autobiography, Reagan outlines his style: "I don't believe a chief executive should supervise every detail of what goes on in his organization. The chief executive should set broad policy and general ground rules, tell people what he or she wants them to do, then let them do it; he should make himself (or *herself*) available, so that the members of his team can come to him if there is a problem. If there is, you can work on it together and, if necessary, fine-tune the policies. But I don't think a chief executive should peer constantly over the shoulders of the people who are in charge of a project and tell them every few minutes what to do."[51]

Anderson writes that Reagan was successful during his first term of office because he set priorities and tried to accomplish one major goal at a time. He first sought to rebuild the country's military strength, then its economic strength. Other major issues were put aside until those tasks were completed: "Those policy priorities set, he handpicked key people to implement them, and delegated the authority and responsibility to get the job done. He seemed to do it easily, without any apparent soul-searching or intellectual struggle, almost as if by instinct."[52]

This style of management works with a competent staff whose members are willing to work with executives and keep them informed about their activities. Anderson proposes that Reagan's style involved a great deal of risk: "When it works, it is spectacular. When it fails, it is also spectacular."[53]

The Road to Bergen-Belsen and Bitburg

Reagan faced many challenging situations during his years as president, but few were more difficult than the events surrounding his European visit in April and May 1985. On November 30, 1984, Reagan met with West Germany's chancellor, Helmut Kohl, in Washington, D.C. Kohl "stressed the importance that West Germans attached to having a part in the fortieth anniversary commemoration of V-E Day [Victory in Europe], especially since West Germany had been excluded in 1984 from the Western Allies' fortieth anniversary celebration of D-Day [the landing of allied troops in France]." In 1984, Kohl and President

Francois Mitterand of France had traveled to the World War I battlefield at Verdun, a visit that "had been so diplomatically successful that Kohl sought to emulate it by encouraging Reagan to visit a German military cemetery with him to signify reconciliation between West Germany and the United States." Reagan was scheduled to attend the annual Western Economic Summit in Germany, an event being hosted by Kohl. Reagan accepted Kohl's invitation to lay a wreath at the military cemetery near Bitburg, the site of a large U.S. Air Force base.[54]

Reagan agreed to participate in the ceremony in order to strengthen relationships between the United States and West Germany, relationships that he believed were crucial to building and maintaining a united opposition to the Soviet Union. Opposition to the Soviet Union was one of Reagan's core beliefs and a theme that he had proclaimed in his rhetoric for more than three decades. Kohl had agreed to deploy U.S. Pershing missiles in Germany in 1983, so Reagan may have been trying to return a favor. Reagan accepted the invitation, according to historian Douglas Brinkley, because of his concern "about keeping Bonn vigilant in the Cold War showdown with the Soviet Union."[55] Reagan was concerned that the Soviet Union was attempting to weaken or split NATO. West Germany was vital to that organization, so Reagan wanted to make sure its leaders knew they had his strong support in opposing the Soviet Union.[56]

Reagan's visit was scheduled during West Germany's elections, and the cemetery at Bitburg was in a region crucial to the electoral success of Kohl's party.[57] The announcement of Reagan's commitment led to outcries from members of the Jewish community, veterans groups, and members of Congress, particularly after the discovery that the Bitburg cemetery contained the graves of German soldiers who served in the Waffen SS, a notorious unit that had committed many atrocities during World War II. After much discussion, Reagan reaffirmed his decision to visit the cemetery, but he later added a stop at the site of the Bergen-Belsen concentration camp in an attempt to silence, or at least weaken, his opposition. He scheduled a speech at Bergen-Belsen and another at the U.S. Air Force base in Bitburg later on the same day after his visit to the cemetery.

One year earlier, in June 1984, Reagan had traveled to Normandy and delivered two highly emotional and successful speeches commemorating the fortieth anniversary of the D-Day invasion—one at Pointe du Hoc and one at Omaha Beach. Ken Duberstein, a former White House chief of staff, once stated that, "as president, Ronald Reagan, delivered three unforgettable speeches: Pointe du Hoc, the *Challenger* disaster,[58] and the Berlin-tear-down-this-wall number.[59] But it was the first of these—Pointe du Hoc—that set the tone for the others."[60] Because that speech was so successful, it can be used as a touchstone to which other ceremonial speeches can be compared.

Brinkley proposes that in his European travels and speeches Reagan "constantly evoked the need to reenergize the grand anti-Fascist alliance of 1941–1945, which led to victory in World War II. Only this time around, Reagan believed, the global democratic crusade had a new enemy: the Soviet Union (a.k.a. the Evil Empire)." In his speech honoring the 2nd Ranger Battalion, a group of volunteers who climbed the cliffs at Pointe du Hoc on June 6, 1944, Reagan "was paying tribute to an entire generation," and he became the spokesperson for that generation of soldiers, a generation that since has been labeled "The Greatest Generation."[61]

Reagan's speeches at Pointe du Hoc and Omaha Beach "were Reagan's signature moments."[62] Brinkley suggests that those speeches "played a seminal role in launching the great reappreciation of World War II veterans that swept over America in the 1980s and continues today largely unabated." He also writes that Reagan's use of visual imagery helped him connect with the veterans: "There was the moving visual of Reagan walking with Nancy amongst all the grave sites, which looked like miles and miles of white crosses. That was an unforgettable moment of absolute reverence for the World War II vets."[63] Cannon proposes that "Reagan's performance at Normandy demonstrated the timing, dramatic sense and attention to detail" for "which the White House staff was famous during his presidency."[64] Brinkley also believes that the speeches and their powerful images were significant factors in Reagan's reelection in 1984. The pictures and words of that day were used in campaign materials during the election.

Observers argued that the emotions Reagan projected at Pointe du Hoc and Omaha Beach were expressions of his true feelings. He was a member of the World War II generation. He served in the Army in World War II although he never left the United States during the war. Rather, he worked in Los Angeles making training and propaganda films. Reagan's patriotism allowed him to offer his "sacramental vision of America,"[65] and he was able to serve as a secular pastor to the country and to the soldiers who fought in World War II and their families. He was in his element, delivering an emotional speech in the kind of situation in which he excelled.

Unfortunately, much of the goodwill created on June 6, 1984, was destroyed by Reagan's acceptance of the invitation by Chancellor Kohl to visit Bitburg cemetery. As Brinkley observes, "He almost lost credibility with members of the 'we' generation over a controversial trip to West Germany."[66] Cannon builds on Brinkley's suggestion: "The Bitburg trip was the unwitting child of Reagan's most successful journey—his commemorative D-Day visit to Normandy in 1984. Kohl had been dismayed by his exclusion from this ceremony. When he came to the White House on November 30, 1984, Kohl gave what was described to me as a tearful account of how he and French President Francois Mitterrand had visited the graves of German and French soldiers at Verdun in World War I and urged Reagan to participate in a similar ceremony of reconciliation honoring the military dead of World War II."[67]

Reagan accepted the invitation to lay a wreath in the cemetery, but he "did not know that the Verdun analogy was inapplicable because there are no German military cemeteries in which both U.S. and German soldiers were buried." Cannon continues, "If Kohl knew this, he did not tell Reagan. Nor did anyone else inform him of this vital fact before the trip was announced the following spring."[68] This lack of information was to cause Reagan significant problems that could have been averted had he been more questioning and concerned or his staff more alert to potential problems.

The ceremonial events at Normandy in 1984 and Germany in 1985 can, then, be linked. One was a tremendous success, the other a troubling event that scarred Reagan's reputation and was the first of several such White House missteps in Reagan's second term.

Reagan's Journey from Dixon to the White House

Reagan's Midwestern roots help explain a great deal about his view of the world and his personality. Although he was born in Tampico, Illinois, and lived in many small towns in the state, Dixon, Illinois, provided Reagan with his roots and many of his values: "We arrived there in 1920 when I was nine years old, and to me it was heaven. Dixon had a busy main street lined with shops, several churches, an elementary and a high school, a public library, a post office, a wire screen factory, a shoe factory, and a cement plant. At the outskirts of town, dairy farms stretched as far as you could see. It was a small universe where I learned standards and values that would guide me for the rest of my life."[69]

Reagan believed that Dixon shaped him in other significant ways. Many people observed that it was really not possible to get to know Reagan because he had built a barrier between himself and the rest of the world. Noonan, like many others who worked with Reagan, never really understood him: "He gleams; he is a mystery. He is for everyone there, for everyone who worked with him. None of them understand him. In private they admit it. You say to them, Who was that masked man?, and they shrug, and hypothesize."[70] One aide wondered if the roots of Reagan's isolation could be linked to some significant event that occurred when he was young: "I think he must have suffered a terrible hurt in his youth, because he closed himself off. He didn't become involved with people. The people he worked with, they were all interchangeable. He didn't become immersed in their lives, and they didn't touch his. He was closed off."[71]

In his autobiography, Reagan attempts to explain this aspect of his personality: "Although I always had lots of playmates, during those first years in Dixon I was a little introverted and probably a little slow in making really close friends. In some ways I think this reluctance to get close to people never left me completely. I've never had trouble making friends, but I've been inclined to hold back a little of myself, reserving it for myself."[72]

Another aspect of Reagan's early life may provide insight into his inability or unwillingness to be open with people. His father Jack was an alcoholic, and like many children of alcoholics Ronald may have learned to cover his true feelings and present a pleasant image to the world rather than confront his father. Cannon did extensive research on children of alcoholics in order to understand and then explain Reagan and his behavior. He was convinced that much of Reagan's personality could be traced to having lived with alcoholism in his family.

In his autobiography, Reagan mentions an event that stuck with him all his life and is cited in many books about him. When he was eleven years old, he came home from the YMCA on a cold winter night. No one was home. As he approached the family home, he found his father "lying in the snow, his arms outstretched, flat on his back. I leaned over to see what was wrong and smelled whiskey. He had found his way home from a speakeasy and had just passed out right there. For a moment or two, I looked down at him and thought about continuing on into the house and going to bed, as if he weren't there. But I couldn't do it. When I tried to wake him he just snored—loud enough, I suspected, for the whole neighborhood to hear him. So I grabbed a piece of his overcoat, pulled it, and dragged him into the house, then put him to bed and never mentioned the incident to my mother."[73]

Cannon writes that events of this kind make it difficult for children of alcoholics to trust people, so they often are unwilling to be themselves and be open to others. Cannon's description fits Reagan perfectly. Others like Peggy Noonan explain that children of alcoholics have a difficult time with intimate relationships, so they end up assuming roles in their homes to cover their pain. She believes that one on the roles Reagan assumed was that it was his job "to cheer everyone up," so he became an entertainer and used his humor to make people feel better.[74]

Although Reagan had some difficult times in Dixon, he came to the conclusion that growing up in a small town could be an advantage for politicians. His description creates the image of an ideal America, the kind of America Reagan often describes in his public discourse: "I think growing up in a small town is a good foundation for anyone who decides to enter politics. You get to know people as individuals, not as blocs or members of special interest groups. You discover that, despite their differences, most people have a lot in common: Every individual is unique, but we all want freedom and liberty, peace, love and security, a good home, and a chance to worship God in our own way; we all want the chance to get ahead and make our children's lives better than our own. We all want the chance to work at a job of our own choosing and to be fairly rewarded for it and the opportunity to control our own destiny."[75]

Reagan's rise from a poor boy in Illinois to the presidency of the United States was very much a part of his own myth and also the myth that anyone in the United States, no matter their roots, can become president of the United States. After completing public schools, Reagan entered Eureka College, a Disciples of Christ college, in Illinois. In the summer he worked as a lifeguard on the Rock River near Dixon, where he is credited with rescuing seventy-seven people in the six years he worked there.[76] Although he was not a sterling student, Reagan was active in drama, sports, and politics.

During his career at Eureka College, Reagan had his first experience in moving an audience to action when he spoke in favor of a student strike against a series of unpopular actions taken by the college president. There has been considerable debate over Reagan's role in the strike; nonetheless, the speech he delivered became significant in his own memory: "I discovered that night that an audience has a feel to it and, in the parlance of the theatre, that audience and I were together."[77] It would be the first of many times that Reagan would have that feeling.

Reagan graduated in 1932, during the Great Depression when there were few opportunities. He found a job as a sportscaster for a radio station in Des Moines, Iowa, and became particularly adept at recreating baseball games from a telegraph relay. That ability to create an image of a real game even though he was in a radio studio obviously was useful training for speaking off the cuff and for saving himself in difficult speaking situations.[78] Reagan became a local celebrity but eventually decided that he wanted to become an actor: "I spoke at quite a few banquets at that time. Some of the material was a bit corny but it did get laughs. I received such a kick out of hearing and seeing audiences react to my talks that I made up my mind to become an actor."[79] This choice of career was not a surprise; Reagan had been involved in theatrical productions since he was a child.

In 1937, Reagan convinced his station's management to send him to California to cover spring training for the Chicago Cubs. While in Los Angeles he was able to get a screen test from Warner Brothers. That screen test led to a contract, and he moved to Los Angeles.[80]

Reagan appeared in more than fifty motion pictures in his career. He was a successful actor but never achieved the critical acclaim he sought. He made many speeches during those years while on publicity tours and during personal appearances. During World War II he served in the military, making training films and serving as a narrator and actor. After the war he became a spokesman for the motion picture industry, primarily through his positions with the Screen Actors Guild. He served on the Guild's board of directors and was its president for seven terms. Many of his speeches during that period were attempts to improve the public image of the movie industry. He was active in trying to rid Hollywood of "alleged Communist influences." He spoke often at public meetings and before congressional committees, thus refining his skills as an orator. He also entered the political arena, giving speeches in support of Democratic politicians and liberal organizations.[81]

After the war, Reagan's movie career waned but he was able to move to a new career in television, a medium he used successfully for the rest of his life. In 1954 he became the host and an actor on *General Electric Theater* and later *Death Valley Days*. He was as a spokesperson for General Electric during the 1950s and 1960s. In that position he gave some nine thousand speeches to audiences across the country, which helped him develop and refine his skills as an orator. He became more and more conservative as the years went on, moving from a New Deal Liberal to a conservative Republican, and began to speak in support of Republican political candidates.[82]

In 1964, Reagan became a national political figure when he delivered a televised speech titled "A Time for Choosing" in support of the unsuccessful presidential candidacy of Senator Barry Goldwater—a

speech that repeated many of the ideas heard in earlier versions of
"The Speech" delivered thousands of times. The speech did not help
Goldwater's campaign, but it was well received throughout the country. A group of wealthy California businessmen were impressed and
began pressing Reagan to run for governor of California in 1966. He
eventually accepted their offer and defeated Edmund G. "Pat" Brown,
a two-term governor. Brown underestimated Reagan and belittled
him as an actor. This approach failed and Reagan won the election by
a wide margin. He was reelected in 1970. He first ran for president in
1968 and continued to campaign for the presidency until his election
in 1980.[83]

Ritter and Henry propose that, during his "odyssey from liberal movie star to conservative president, Ronald Reagan consistently portrayed
himself as a concerned citizen speaking his convictions." During that
time, he spoke as president of the Screen Actors Guild, a spokesperson
for General Electric, and an advocate of conservative causes and candidates. He developed a "rhetoric that was secular and political rather
than religious. His speeches were at once reassuring and alarming, for
he both celebrated traditional American values and warned that they
were in danger of being lost forever. Through such speeches he found
his political voice and his political audience. Eventually they would
take him into political office."[84]

Ritter and Henry describe Reagan's speeches as having three features:
"a general pattern of lamentation—bemoaning America's difficulties
and a warning that the future could hold far worse; the portrayal of a
cosmic struggle between good and evil; and a warning of an impending
political Armageddon and even the possibility of a dark millennium."
But his rhetoric was more negative than most religious rhetoric: "Reagan neglected to portray the glorious rewards that ultimately awaited
the faithful on earth (the millennium) and in heaven. At the same time
... Reagan held out hope that the course of history could be reversed,
that America could save herself."[85] This pattern would continue into his
presidential years. Even in the most difficult periods of his administration, Reagan would always find a reason for hope in a better future.

Reagan's belief in a better future was a natural outgrowth of his optimistic view of the world. For Deaver, "his unwavering optimism changed the way we thought about ourselves and the way the world looked at us."[86]

Cannon builds on Deaver's ideas: "This optimism was not a trivial or peripheral quality. It was the essential ingredient of an approach to life that had carried Reagan from the backwater of Dixon to fame as a sports announcer and then to the stages of Hollywood and of the world. And it was a fundamental component of his idealistic nationalism, expressed best in the phrase he expropriated from Abraham Lincoln that America is 'the last best hope of man on earth.'"[87]

That optimism was reflected in Reagan's most basic beliefs: "I have always wondered at this American marvel, the great energy of the human soul that drives people to better themselves and improve the fortunes of their families and communities. Indeed, I know of no greater force on earth."[88] This great drive would always lead Americans to a better world, and Reagan saw his role as president making it possible for Americans to achieve their goals. Wills argues that the optimism was apparent in his use of a quote by Thomas Paine: "We have it in our power to start the world over." According to Wills, this belief was also exhibited in Reagan's statement during his speeches at Bergen-Belsen and Bitburg: "I don't think we ought to focus on the past. I want to focus on the future."[89]

Reagan as Storyteller

Rhetorical critic Paul D. Erickson argues that "the overarching theme of Reagan's rhetoric has been a restoration of our communal beliefs," like "a restoration of national self-confidence in domestic and foreign affairs" and "having faith in the American Dream, that curious and variously defined myth of America that holds we are a chosen people, blessed by God and acting as his agents on earth." Those myths had a powerful function in Reagan's rhetoric and provided him with a series of stories he could use effectively. In his presentations, Reagan would tell a story and then give "an example of how to respond . . . in ideological and emotional terms." Erickson notes that Reagan had a great deal of control over which stories he would tell in his speeches and how he wished those stories to be received: "In moving from the movie screen to the boardroom and podium, Ronald Reagan could in effect become his own author and director. The impulse toward creating a character remained, but came under his own control." One of his most powerful devices was "his use of stock symbolic characters": "By personifying his beliefs about good and evil in simply drawn men and women, the President provides points of reference and points of view for his audience.... The heroes and villains of Reagan's speeches are far from realistic; they are tools through which the speaker manipulates us by translating our complicated and varied lives into stock characters." Reagan's heroes were not the great figures in society but average individuals: "If unquestioning faith is the characteristic virtue of Reagan's heroes, then intellectual skepticism is the hubristic sin that can bring the world down in ruin. Reagan's villains are intellectuals who presume superiority over the man of common sense because intellectuals, supposedly, assume that they are, to put it bluntly, smarter. These include academics, intellectuals, professional politicians, and, of course, communists."[90]

Reagan consistently proclaimed that the average American was wiser and more intelligent than politicians and intellectuals. His stories dramatically illustrated that belief. Robinson suggests that Reagan's stories were successful because he reaffirmed the role of ordinary citizens in politics: "Bigger government, higher taxes, détente with the Soviet Union—broadly speaking, these had been the policies of experts. Smaller government, lower taxes, and peace through strength—broadly speaking, these had been the policies of ordinary Americans. In championing these simple, commonsense policies, Reagan had returned ordinary Americans to the center of national life." Reagan still relied on experts to create administrative policy, but he also realized that "the insights of ordinary Americans remained just as valid as those of anybody else."[91]

Reagan's Humor

In addition to being an adept storyteller, Reagan possessed a sense of humor that he used successfully in his daily life and his speeches. "He was the resident humorist and gag writer in a White House where nearly everything else was done for him while he engaged in governance by anecdote. While adversaries interpreted his heavy reliance on anecdotes as a telltale reflection of a deficient intellect, Reagan treasured humorous stories and knew that his willingness to poke fun at himself was a vital component of his popularity. A sense of humor was essential to the role Reagan had created for himself in Hollywood and politics and, in humorist Bob Orben's phrase, the basis for the 'balance of goodwill' upon which he drew in time of trouble."[92]

His use of humor in the White House may have been a vehicle to take a break from the daily political battles. According to Cannon, "Reagan quipped, kidded, and bantered in nearly every White House meeting, charming visitors and aides alike." He also used humor to create links to the White House staff: "During his eight years in the White House he won the allegiance of subordinates and secretaries with endless banter and little jokes that reassured them and made them feel part of a great enterprise. These quips and banter enabled Reagan to keep his emotional distance from his entourage while also giving the White House rank and file a sense of belonging."[93]

The Actor President

One of the most common perceptions associated with Reagan is that he was playing the role of president. As a former actor, Reagan had internalized the idea that life was a role he had to play. Noonan describes this aspect of his life: "I used to see him walking through the halls, putting his hands together in the fighter's victory clasp, waving up at us in the old Executive Office Building, nodding as he left the reception. I would wonder, What does he feel? This man of awesome cool warmth, so friendly and so remote, who in the eighth decade still roused himself each morning for the role and all its rigors—who was he?"[94]

She elaborates and describes the actor coming out in Reagan's role as president: "He didn't work from the inside out, he worked from the outside in. He saw his role and put it on, like a costume. He had respect for the set and respect for the character he played, or rather the title and circumstances of the character. He really always played himself; the vivid have no choice. That's why he seemed both phony and authentic. Because he was. He was really acting but the part he played was Ronald Reagan."[95]

Gergen also discusses the issue of Reagan's training as an actor and its effect on his job as president. He writes that Reagan's training as an actor taught him to "commit what he read to memory—he had a steel-trap mind for such things—but as a result, he also read very slowly. We had learned, just as his aides did when he was governor of California, not to give him too much to read at night because he would stay up too late." Gergen concludes that theatrical talent was helpful to a presidential speaker and summarizes the image of Reagan as a successful leader/speaker: "What Reagan had—an engaging style, a guiding philosophy, an inspiring story, an enveloping humor, a theatrical touch—he put to good use."[96]

Reagan believed that his acting provided him skills that would be useful as a politician. He claims that on many occasions he was asked, "How could an actor be president?" He responded with a standard answer, "I've sometimes wondered how you could be president and not be an actor." He argued that an actor must understand the motivations of the character he is playing. In doing that, he learns to put himself in the shoes of the other person: "The process, called empathy, is not bad for someone who goes into politics (or any other calling). By developing a knack for putting yourself in someone else's shoes, it helps you relate better to others and perhaps understand why they think as they do, even though they come from a background much different from yours."[97]

Tony Dolan, one of Reagan's speechwriters, proposes that Reagan's acting career was helpful because "actors get used to the idea of alternative endings. . . . Scenes can be rewritten. New endings can be added." Actors have to know how to stand before a camera and deliver their lines, but they also must have an imagination. Dolan explains: "He has to be able to size up a script. . . . Reagan can imagine a post-Soviet world—he can really *see* it. So he tossed out the old script to write a new script of his own. What the Gipper likes is happy endings, not tragedies."[98]

CHAPTER 2

Reagan as Ceremonial Speaker

Ronald Reagan was a successful presidential orator in many settings and on many occasions, but he was often particularly effective in ceremonial situations. Because this book focuses on two significant ceremonial speeches, I begin this chapter with a discussion of ceremonial speaking and the expectations of speakers and audiences in ceremonial settings.

Ceremonial Oratory

Scholars have long attempted to define the essential characteristics of epideictic, or ceremonial, oratory. The traditional definition centers around issues of "praise or blame of an object, event or person."[1] Some researchers view this definition as being too limited, however, because many types of speech deal with issues of praise and blame.

Rhetorical critics Waldo W. Braden and Harold Mixon propose that epideictic speeches are "a celebration of communal values and traditional beliefs and feelings of the listeners." The ceremonial speaker "draws upon those values and concepts that his auditors [listeners] already accept" and builds upon and amplifies them in the speech.[2] Reagan often spoke of traditional values and beliefs in ceremonial speeches, but he used similar appeals in other speaking situations as well.

Braden and Mixon also state that successful ceremonial speakers use myths that are believed and accepted by the audience and therefore appeal to the communal values expressed by those myths. They believe that the content of the speech "is controlled by the occasion, which limits what is appropriate for the speaker to say and do."[3] Rhetorical critic Bonnie Dow agrees when she argues that epideictic speeches "allow the audience to reach a communal understanding of the events which have occurred." She further proposes that the speech must "be placed in a context that aligns it with past experiences and the beliefs and values that govern [the audience's] understanding of such experiences." The speaker should define the audience's role in response to the situation.[4] The speaker must be conscious of the nature of the occasion and the audience expectations of what should be said on that occasion. A speaker who violates those expectations may be rejected by the audience.

Braden and Mixon also propose that ceremonial speaking can go beyond its traditional purpose and offer the audience "a course of action . . . for the future."[5] As Mary Stuckey writes, Reagan tried to unite everyone into a "single 'American' audience."[6] Once he created the audience, he could call upon that united group to follow his suggestions on future actions or support a policy he proposed.

In the most extensive study of ceremonial speaking by a communication scholar, Celeste Condit outlines three paired functions of epideictic speaking: understanding and definition, sharing and creation of community, and entertainment and display. The first term of the pair indicates the speaker's function and the second the audience's function in the ceremonial setting. In the definition/understanding function, the speaker "will explain the troubling issue in terms of the audience's key values and beliefs." If successful, "the troubling event will be made less confusing and threatening, providing a sense of comfort for the audience." The speaker will gain the power to define.[7]

In the shaping/sharing of community function, the speaker develops and maintains a sense of community. Communities "need to have explicit definitions of major shared experiences," symbols, values, myths, and heritage. If change occurs, "the community renews its conception of itself and what is good by explaining what it has previously held to be good and by working through the relationships of those past values and beliefs to new situations." If audience members object to values stated in a speech, "the result is likely to be a sense of alienation from the community."[8]

Ceremonial speeches often "invite the speaker to display his or her eloquence." Condit describes eloquence as a "combination of truth, beauty, and power in human speech, and is a unique capacity of humanity." Members of the audience are entertained in a "humane manner" and are "allowed to stretch their daily experiences into meaning more grand, sweet, noble, or delightful." The audience also "judges the display of the speaker, because the speaker may well present eloquence as a means of self promotion." The audience may take eloquence to be "a sign of leadership."[9]

According to Condit, speakers can mold audiences and define the "public destiny," but "it is equally true that audiences mold speakers and the public destiny as well." She continues: "The constraints of the audience's needs, its willingness to call for a speaker and to listen, its demands that the orator speak for all the people and use the people's values and heritage place powerful limits on how far the speaker can take the audience, and how events can be explained." In the end, epideictic speeches "maintain community values" but also can "accomplish the progressive function of adapting our community to new times, technologies, geographies, and events."[10]

Reagan's Ceremonial Speaking

Reagan's ceremonial speeches contained many of the themes that formed the essence of his public messages: He looked to the past with nostalgia for a simpler, easier world while projecting a future full of peace, justice, and happiness. Kurt Ritter and David Henry argue that Reagan was a successful epideictic orator because of his ability "to imbue secular political events and issues with the trappings of religious ritual" in combination with "his undeniably appealing delivery skills." Ceremonial situations gave Reagan a forum to emphasize "the most salient features" of his rhetoric, including "unself-conscious references to God, emphasis on heroes, appeals to values of freedom and progress, and Reagan's fitting presentational manner." In Reagan's ceremonial speeches, "he created miniature dramas populated with Americans who embodied his message of individualism and conservative values."[11]

Ceremonial occasions provided Reagan opportunities to include stories as a crucial part of his message in settings that were often chosen by his advisors because they evoked powerful visual imagery for television. The visual images heightened the power of his stories and his message. Reagan's staff, especially during his first term, was adept at finding such settings. Reagan was so successful in his use of television, write Ritter and Henry, that he "has become the benchmark for a media communicator; he is the standard against which other politicians will be measured."[12]

William F. Lewis argues that Reagan's success as speaker can best be "seen and judged" by analyzing his ability to tell stories. According to Lewis, "Stories are not just a rhetorical device that Reagan uses to embellish his ideas; Reagan's message is a story. Reagan uses story-telling to direct his policies, ground his explanations, and inspire his audiences, and the dominance of narrative helps to account for the variety of reactions to his rhetoric."[13] One of Reagan's aides, Lyn Nofziger, expressed the importance of stories in Reagan's mind: "Truth is not the same thing to him as to you and me. If Ronald Reagan tells a story three times it becomes true, at least to him."[14] Those who accepted the truth of his stories agreed with his message, but those who could not believe that his stories were realistic rejected his message.[15]

According to Lewis, Reagan told two kinds of stories: anecdotes that "define the character of an issue at the same time they illustrate, reinforce, and make his policies more vivid," and myth that "structures his message." Anecdotes are "quick stories, jokes, or incidents that are the verbal counterpart of the visual image." Lewis defines myths as "any anonymously composed story telling of origins and destinies: the explanations a society offers its young of why the world is and why we do as we do, its pedagogic image of the nature and destiny" of people. For Lewis, "myth provides a sense of importance and direction and it provides a communal focus for individual identity."[16]

Lewis summarizes the myth that was present in virtually all of Reagan's rhetoric: "America is a chosen nation, grounded in its families and neighborhoods, and driven inevitably forward by its heroic working people toward a world of freedom and economic progress unless blocked by moral or military weakness. . . . It is a story that is sanctified by God and validated by the American experience." Lewis explains how Reagan's myth was such a powerful part of his rhetoric: "The story fulfills all the requirements of myth—it is widely believed, generally unquestioned and clearly pedagogical. And Reagan tells the story extremely well." He concludes, "For Reagan, America's meaning is to be found as much in the future as it has been in the past," so his myths look to a better world in the future.[17]

According to Lewis, Reagan's stories "define what it means to be an American." Individuals who listen to Reagan's speeches are "encouraged to see himself or herself as a central actor in America's quest for freedom." Reagan also plays a major role in the story as "a mythic hero" who "embodies the role of the compassionate, committed political outsider; he is the active force that has arrived to help right the prevailing wrongs and to get things moving again. As the narrator of the story, Reagan is portrayed as simply presenting the nature of the situation. There is no artifice and no threat in this style of realistic narration; Reagan-as-narrator just presents things as they are." The stories are not used to call attention to Reagan but to support the ideas and arguments that make up his worldview.[18]

Reagan's use of story was successful when his narrative was consistent with the beliefs of his audience. Lewis proposes that the "stories that have caused the most trouble for Reagan are those which are least in accord with the generally accepted understanding" of his audience. He uses the address at Bitburg Air Base as an example. Reagan's trouble at Bitburg, he claims, "stemmed from his account contradicting the received understanding of America waging war to destroy the evils of Nazi conquest."[19]

Davis Houck and Amos Kiewe extend Lewis's ideas by arguing that Reagan used stories in a manner that was different from most speakers: "Instead of his stories functioning as anecdotal evidence for some broad claim, these stories functioned more as truths in Reagan's rhetorical schema. . . . Since the grounds for his claims were often surreptitiously embedded in his stories, only a competing story with different characters could effectively refute Reagan on his terms." They also agree with Lewis that at times Reagan becomes the hero of his own narrative.[20]

Ritter and Henry outline why Reagan used heroes so often in his stories: "They exemplified the American community's values of generosity, kindness, and volunteer action. Like the heroes of individualism, these heroes acted as private citizens; they needed no government agency. Their generosity stretched from small-town America to the entire world."[21] Reagan believed that average citizens were wiser and more moral than individuals who worked in government or intellectuals, so he used them as a model of the good in society. He also praised people who lived in small towns like those where he grew up in Illinois.

Historian Garry Wills provides insights into Reagan's use of stories in which he took large events and focused them on one individual: "Even when Reagan had genuine stories to tell, genuine heroes to celebrate, he casts a mythic, even religious aura over them, and makes complex operations the story of one man. So, at the Normandy ceremony of June 6, 1984, Operation Overlord became the tale of Private Zanatta, told in the moving words of his daughter, who was present on camera [at Reagan's speech at Omaha Beach]."[22]

Wills observes that Reagan's discussion of the Holocaust during his speeches in Germany during the Bitburg controversy boiled down to the story of one individual, Adolph Hitler. At Bergen-Belsen and Bitburg, when he talked about the evil actions of Hitler and other Nazis during World War II, Reagan saw "issues in moral terms, where the choice is clear. This means that the evil is always undiluted."[23] Communication critic John Murphy agrees with Wills when he observes that ceremonial speaking "is concerned with issues of honor and dishonor; all other concerns fade before this issue."[24]

Wills believes that Reagan was an effective ceremonial speaker because he loved the ceremonial role a president played and preferred situations where he could give speeches to the day-to-day tasks necessary in running a presidential office: "Reagan clearly relishes the ceremonial aspects of his office, and multiplies them, finding new occasions to give out medals, awards, presidential congratulations: attending as many banquets and memorial functions as he can fit into a schedule that is notoriously light on desk hours; getting as much television coverage at these events as at political jobs more narrowly defined."[25]

Reagan as Orator

An underlying idea to this point is that one of, if not the most important part of, the Reagan presidency was his ability to appeal to an audience through public speaking. Many authors have attempted to explain what made Reagan a successful speaker. Lou Cannon states that Reagan had an inner need to speak to audiences: "He delighted in the roar of a crowd and could become distracted and listless if kept too long away from audiences."[26] Reagan's aides were aware of his needs and provided him many situations in which he could meet with and speak to audiences.

Cannon also points out the consistency in Reagan's public discourse: "Reagan had a knack for incorporating his experiences into a universal message and explaining large matters in simple ways. His critics complained that he oversimplified, resorting too often to anecdotes, but most of Reagan's stories had a purpose." He describes the sources and themes of Reagan's speeches: "Over time he came to a few settled beliefs and wrote them down in speeches, sprinkled with odd anecdotes. He found his arguments and his anecdotes in *Reader's Digest* and in newspaper stories and rarely questioned their validity. He preached love of country, distrust of government, the glories of economic opportunity, the dangers of regulating business, and the wonders of free markets and free trade. He believed in the manifest destiny of the United States of America. He also believed in intuition, psychic phenomena and fate. He was fascinated by the biblical story of Armageddon."[27]

Cannon and others believe that much of Reagan's success as a speaker can be directly linked to his training as an actor. The title of Cannon's biography, *President Reagan: The Role of a Lifetime,* signals the belief that much of Reagan's political life was really a continuation of his life as an actor. Cannon borrows a quote from Reagan to illustrate this point: "Some of my critics over the years have said that I became president because I was an actor who knew how to give a good speech. I suppose that's not too far wrong. Because an actor knows two important things—to be honest in what he is doing and to be in touch with the audience. That's not bad advice for a politician either. My actor's instinct simply told me to speak the truth as I saw it and felt it."[28]

Cannon then interprets Reagan: "The last phrase is interesting because what Reagan saw and felt as an actor frequently did not correspond to the facts. Reagan recognized this, and in a conflict between feelings and facts, usually gave greater weight to his feelings. If an actor did not believe in his part, no one else would believe in it. If a political speaker did not believe in his message, he could not persuade others of its merits."[29]

Cannon continues his explanation of the relevance of Reagan's experiences as an actor to his public speaking, particularly on television: "Since Reagan was convinced that the camera invariably detects insincerity, his adage about speaking the truth as he saw and felt it applied with special force whenever he appeared on television. Reagan always believed what he was saying, even when the message was not strictly factual. He believed in the power of stories, sincerely told. And he was convinced that the actor's truth he had discovered for himself applied in some measure to everyone. This made him sympathetic to others when they also told cherished stories that reflected feelings more than facts."[30]

During the years when he was a representative for General Electric, Reagan developed his standard message and method of speaking. He found that he was not able to keep an audience's attention when reading his speech, so he developed a technique that he used for the rest of his life: "I began listing the main points I want to make in a speech on four-by-six inch cards with abbreviations for some words: 'That,' for example, became 'tht,' 'barren desert' would be 'barrn dsrt.' Just the letters told me what the word was, and usually other words in a sentence would be so obvious to me when I looked down at the card,

I'd remember the rest. I might include three of four words to remind me of a story or joke that I wanted to tell, then I'd ad lib the rest."[31]

Martin Anderson suggests that Reagan's technique made it appear as though he were speaking impromptu. In reality, Reagan had a set of note cards in his pocket that he would carefully remove so that the audience could not readily see them, and he would then speak from those notes in an extemporaneous manner. Reagan was so deft at looking at his notes that most members of the audience were not aware he was using them. Reagan had weak eyesight, so he wore contact lenses. He developed the technique of taking the contact out of his right eye and using that eye to read from the note cards. He used his left eye to maintain eye contact with his audience. This technique obviously would be extremely difficult to perform, but he perfected it after years of practice.[32]

Reagan learned to use eye contact with audience members as a source of feedback about how his message was being received: "He attaches on people. There could be 15,000 people in the audience. He will attach on one person and another, but he will watch their reaction personally to what he is saying."[33] Peter Hannaford, a Reagan speechwriter, explains Reagan's extension of this practice to television. When he spoke on television, Reagan knew "that when he looked into the camera, he was really looking at one person, or one family, seated before a set in the living room. What he would have with them was a quiet conversation, just as if he was in the living room with them."[34] Reagan describes his relationship with the audience: "When I'm speaking to a crowd—or on television—I try to remember that audiences are made up of individuals and I try to speak as if I am talking to a group of friends . . . not to millions, but to a handful of people in a living room . . . or a barbershop."[35]

Reagan kept refining his public speaking techniques throughout his career. Kenneth Khachigian, the main author of the Bergen-Belsen speech, said that Reagan never stopped analyzing how to communicate his vision more effectively: "He is always thinking."[36]

In a careful analysis of Reagan as a presidential orator, David Gergen proposes that he was successful because "every good leader is good on stage." Reagan was able to make people relax and open their minds to his words, he talked about great ideas in an effective manner, he used well-chosen stories that were a form of moral instruction that captured large truths, he embodied his message, he kept the focus on others and not himself, he drew upon communal experiences, and he used humor effectively. Gergen also outlines the tricks of the speech trade Reagan had learned: prepare carefully, keep it short, keep it brisk, use the language of the living room, use catchy facts, occasionally use props, be positive, anticipate the critics, and have a good closer.[37] Anderson adds another of Reagan's strengths to Gergen's list: "He became especially skillful at taking complex, difficult policy issues, extracting the essence of the idea, and then translating that essence into clear, vivid language that almost everyone could understand."[38]

Peter Robinson adds that humor was crucial in Reagan's speaking: Humor "produced a larger and more important effect as well. It reassured people. It made them feel better. When Reagan told a joke, he wasn't trying to make an audience like him, but giving it a gift. He was reaching into that zone deep within himself that was somehow always filled with delight . . . to give his listeners a little delight of their own. Humor, he saw, provided a kind of universal solvent, capable of washing cares away, and he always took the time to make people feel better." Humor was another way Reagan's optimism came through in his speeches. Robinson observes that Reagan taught him "to appreciate the *meaning* of humor. The world contains more good than bad, more courage than cowardice, and more reason for smiles than tears. Laughter is a profession of faith."[39]

Rhetorical critic John Meyer proposes that Reagan used humor in virtually every speech he made "to make a point persuasively" while at the "same time entertaining or ingratiating [himself with] his audience." Reagan chose humor as a vehicle to reduce tension between himself and audiences, put the audience at ease in tense situations and "increase their confidence in him," lighten the mood of the occasion, make it easier for him to discuss controversial topics, describe the irrational acts of his opponents and ridicule them, provide him a weapon to be "used in political infighting," "establish a sense of equality with the audience" by showing that he was not superior to them, and show ways the audience was superior to others, including his political opponents and intellectuals. Meyer concludes: "Humor is an important tool for the process of ingratiation, as humor has been found to cause people to look more objectively at an issue which is laughed at, as well as making them feel good about a speaker personally, and to build and reinforce actual support for his or her position."[40]

Reagan's Speechwriters

After he became president, Reagan did not have time to write his own messages, so he had to rely on speechwriters: "Though most of his speeches were written by others, many of them still reflected the uncluttered values he had expressed on the banquet circuit for a quarter century."[41] Because Reagan's views were so well known, the speechwriters had a ready supply of ideas and language they could use to draft the message. Still, though Reagan did not write the speeches, he provided significant input into the ideas and the language of some, though not all, of his public addresses.

Peggy Noonan, the author of the Pointe du Hoc speech, describes the role of the presidential speechwriter in some detail: "Speechwriting is an odd profession, part policy-explainer, part hack, part . . . what? Innocent in a way, for speechwriters, no matter how long in the game, have to continue being moved as if for the first time by things like democracy; and speechwriters are, somehow, the kids of politics, itself in some ways a kid's game. Prohibited from policy, temperamentally unsuited, many of them, to political leadership, and consigned to a city that both esteems and dislikes writers, a city of powerful men on the Hill, in the agencies, who are often inarticulate and who dislike being reminded of their condition by the presence of a pale and nervous wordsmith—that's what they call them, wordsmiths."[42]

All the same, Noonan argues, what speechwriters do is important. "I don't mean to make too much of it—rhetoric is only a small stream off the river of American prose—but in terms of politics it is the ocean you sail on or sink in."[43] Skilled speechwriters were crucial for a president like Ronald Reagan because so much of his administration was defined by his ability to appeal to the public through the spoken word.

Noonan outlines training herself to become a presidential speechwriter: "In the White House they keep big, thick volumes of the speeches, utterances and meetings with the press of the presidents, all the presidents. I'd take a few volumes from the library upstairs and read them at random. In time I knew I was looking for the grammar of the presidency, the sound and tone and tense of it. And I knew where to go: to the modern president who had sounded most like a president, the one who set the standard for how the rest should sound. I went to FDR."[44]

It is interesting that Noonan studied Franklin D. Roosevelt's speeches, because Roosevelt had a significant effect on Reagan and his rhetoric. When he was younger, Reagan was a strong follower of Roosevelt and his policies. Even after Reagan became a conservative and rejected many of the more liberal policies, he often quoted Roosevelt in his speeches.

In his autobiography, Reagan describes his practice of sitting down with speechwriters and going over the points that he wanted to make in a speech. He gave the speechwriters basic guidelines on his style and technique: "I told them to use some of my rules for speaking: I prefer short sentences; don't use a word with two syllables if a one-syllable word will do; and if you can, use an example. An example is better than a sermon." He also writes about organizing a speech: "My years in show business and the experience of making thousands of speeches over the years probably taught me something about timing and cadence and how to reach an audience. Here's my formula: I usually start with a joke or story to catch the audience's attention; then I tell them what I am going to tell them, I tell them, and then I tell them what I just told them."[45] That advice was a common one that many successful speakers followed and one they were willing to share with people who wanted to improve their speaking.

Robinson describes the length speechwriters went to in applying Reagan's formula: "As a speechwriter, I became an expert on Reagan. All his speechwriters did. It was the only way we could do our work.

We mastered every position he had ever taken, poring over his old speeches, radio talks, and newspaper columns. We scribbled down ever word he uttered when we met with him in the Oval Office. And we watched him work. It was an unwritten rule in the speechwriting shop that whenever the President delivered a speech that you yourself had written, you yourself showed up to observe."[46]

Robinson concludes that the speechwriters "were trying to inhabit Reagan's mind." They were so absorbed with Reagan that they developed imitations of his speaking: "Since it is perfectly possible for words to look just right on paper but sound all wrong spoken aloud, when a speechwriter finished a draft, he would test it by reading passages as if he were the President himself. . . . we all identified with Reagan so completely that when the speechwriter opened his mouth it would be the President's voice that came out." If you looked over the shoulder of six speechwriters, wrote Robinson, you would discover that all of the speeches sounded like Reagan: "It was our job to sound like the President, of course, but that never helped me to understand the way we managed to do so. I felt like an idiot savant. I could perform the trick, but I didn't know how." Reagan himself was often active in the writing: "The President edited every draft the speechwriters sent to him, condensing material, enlivening flat passages, and firming up arguments."[47]

The speechwriters broke their tasks into three parts. On each speech "we'd spend about a third of our time on research, plowing through background reading that included materials on the audience the President would be addressing and on relevant aspects of administration policy." The second third was spent on the difficult process of writing the speech. The speechwriters all followed a pattern when composing text, especially when they had a difficult time writing the speech or faced writer's block. The final third was in staffing—"the process in which each speech was circulated to the senior staff and certain Cabinet agencies." The numerous readers proposed changes, and the speechwriter then spent significant time working with the various groups to achieve agreement on the message.[48]

That part of the job was often frustrating because other readers made suggestions that posed a problem: "Their drafts were drab. They were bureaucratic. They lacked conviction. They failed to match the trumpetlike sound of Ronald Reagan."[49] In the Reagan Library there is a draft of the Bergen-Belsen speech by an unnamed individual in the State Department. Robinson's description is accurate. Although the State Department draft includes many of the ideas eventually included in the Bergen-Belsen speech, it indeed is drab and lifeless. It does not at all sound like Ronald Reagan and would have been a terrible failure if it had been delivered.

Josh Gilder, the author of the Bitburg speech, describes the speechwriting process in the White House as an extremely efficient one in which Reagan was given drafts of all major speeches at least forty-eight hours in advance. Reagan would carefully read a draft and make edits that evening, then return it to the speechwriters, who would send a revised version back to Reagan later that day. Once the text was complete there were very few changes. According to Gilder, Reagan went through each speech text line by line before delivering it. In effect, he practiced every speech, something not every president was willing to do.[50]

Reagan's D-Day Speeches

Even though Reagan claimed to have significant input in his speech drafts, there were many in which he provided little or even met with the speechwriter. A prime example was the Pointe du Hoc speech, written by Peggy Noonan. Gergen describes that speech as the pinnacle of Reagan's speechmaking: "With veterans in front and the sea behind, he described the valor of the men who scaled those sheer, hundred-foot cliffs as German fire cut them to pieces. His audience was moved to tears, and clips will forever be shown in Reagan retrospectives."[51] Gergen was surprised to learn that Reagan had never spoken to Noonan about the speech, she was not present on the occasion, and Reagan not did even meet her until after the speech had been delivered.

When Noonan finally met with Reagan, he was very pleasant but she got the feeling that he did not know why he was meeting with her.

Finally one of his aides mentioned that she had written his Pointe du Hoc speech. He then warmly commended her for the speech: "But it was wonderful. Were you there? Well, after the speech, the original Pointe du Hoc fellows came up and told me how much they liked it, and there were tears in their eyes."[52]

Noonan later described what she learned after composing the text of the Pointe du Hoc speech: "What I learned from the Pointe du Hoc speech was that to the men of the Reagan White House, a good speech is really a sausage skin, the stronger it is the more you shove in." She learned to use the power of the moment and the occasion as a vehicle to produce memorable rhetoric and thought that the commemoration at Pointe du Hoc was an event that could be universalized as a reflection of the human spirit: "The subject matter was one of those moments that really captures the romance of history. I thought that if I could get at what impelled the Rangers to do what they did, I could use it to suggest what impels us each day as we live as a nation in the world. This would remind both us and our allies of what it is that holds us together."[53]

The timing of the speech was controversial. Deaver and others wanted Reagan to speak at 1 P.M. in France so that the speech would appear on morning shows in the United States. The French wanted him to speak after his 4:00 P.M. official greeting ceremony with President Mitterrand. The standoff was eventually resolved, with the speech delivered at the time Reagan's aides desired.[54]

The speech begins with a look back at the world forty years ago: "We're here to mark that day in history when the Allied armies joined in battle to reclaim this continent to liberty. For 4 long years, much of Europe had been under a terrible shadow. Free nations had fallen, Jews cried out in the camps, millions cried out for liberation. Europe was enslaved, and the world prayed for its rescue. Here in Normandy, the rescue began. Here the Allies stood and fought against tyranny in a giant undertaking unparalleled in human history."[55]

Reagan verbally paints a picture of that day in beautiful, descriptive language: "We stand on a lonely, windswept point on the northern shore of France. The air is soft, but 40 years ago at this moment the air was dense with smoke and the cries of men, and the air was filled with the crack of rifle fire and the roar of cannon. At dawn, on the morning of the 6th of June, 1944, 235 Rangers jumped off the British landing craft and ran to the bottom of these cliffs. Their mission was one of the most difficult and daring of the invasion: to climb these sheer and desolate cliffs and take out the enemy guns. The Allies had been told that some of the mightiest of these guns were here and they would be trained on the beaches to stop the Allied advance."

Noonan was able to place the audience at the center of those events through the use of onomatopoeia: "What I was doing here was placing it all in time and space for myself and, by extension, for the audience. If we really listen to and hear the snap of the flag, the reality of that sound—snap . . . suhnapp– will help us imagine what it sounded like on D-Day. And would help us imaging what D-Day itself was like. Then your head snaps back with remembered information: History is real."[56]

Reagan continues to paint his picture with the Rangers climbing rope ladders up the cliff in the face of tremendous opposition by the German soldiers. "One by one, the Rangers pulled themselves over the top, and in seizing the firm land at the top of those cliffs, they began to seize back the continent of Europe. Two hundred and twenty-five came here. After 2 days of fighting, only 90 could still bear arms."

The picture now shifts from the past to the present with a description of the current situation, a visual that was striking on television: "Behind me is a memorial that symbolizes the Ranger daggers that were thrust into the top of these cliffs. And before me are the men who put them there." He describes the surviving Rangers in a series of parallel sentences: "These are the boys of Pointe du Hoc. These are the men who took the cliffs. These are the champions who helped free a continent. These are the heroes who helped end a war."

Reagan next comments that he knows that many of the Rangers were probably thinking, "We were just a part of a bigger effort; everyone was there that day." He answers that thought: "Well, everyone was." He then tells a typical Reagan story in which a specific individual personifies the entire effort: "Do you remember the story of Bill Millin of the 51st

Highlanders? Forty years ago today, British troops were pinned down near a bridge, waiting desperately for help. Suddenly, they heard the sound of bagpipes, and some thought they were dreaming. Well, they weren't. They looked up and saw Bill Millin with his bagpipes, leading the reinforcements and ignoring the smack of the bullets into the ground around him." Again Noonan used words with sound, the bullets "smack" into the ground. The audience can hear the sound and visualize the day. Reagan continues: "Lord Lovat was with him—Lord Lovat of Scotland, who calmly announced when he got to the bridge, 'Sorry I'm a few minutes late,' as if he'd been delayed by a traffic jam, when in truth he had come from the bloody fighting on Sword Beach, which he and his men had just taken."

Reagan continues by describing the heroism of the British troops, the Polish troops, and the Canadians. He then wonders aloud why men would undertake such a difficult mission and then answers his own question by saying that the young men undertook this dangerous task because of "faith and belief; it was loyalty and love." Reagan now becomes a secular preacher to the world and exclaims that the men fought so gallantly because they "had faith that what they were doing was right, faith that they fought for all humanity, faith that a just God would grant them mercy on this beachhead or on the next."

He now turns to one of the myths he used often in his rhetoric, the myth of American uniqueness: "One's country is worth dying for, and democracy is worth dying for, because it's the most deeply honorable form of government ever devised by man. All of you loved liberty. All of you were willing to fight tyranny, and you knew the people of your countries were behind you." Reagan becomes a secular preacher and says that Americans have opposed tyranny in the past and by implication will continue to do so in the future. He continues to preach by noting that the soldiers were being supported by people who were praying for them in Georgia and in Kansas and in Philadelphia. "They were ringing the Liberty Bell." As a preacher, he also recalls the faith of the men who were fighting: "Something else helped the men of D-day: their rockhard belief that Providence would have a great hand in the events that would unfold here; that God was an ally in this great cause. And so, the night before the invasion, when Colonel Wolverton asked his parachute troops to kneel with him in prayer he told them: 'Do not bow your heads, but look up so you can see God and ask His blessing in what we're about to do.' Also that night, General Matthew Ridgway on his cot, listening in the darkness for the promise God made to Joshua: 'I will not fail thee nor forsake thee.'"

Reagan could not have anticipated that a year later General Ridgway would feature significantly in another Reagan speech as a participant in the wreath-laying ceremony at Bitburg cemetery. Nor could he anticipate that his next phrases would be repeated the following year at Bergen-Belsen and Bitburg: "When the war was over, there were lives to be rebuilt and governments to be returned to the people. There were nations to be reborn. Above all, there was a new peace to be assured. These were huge and daunting tasks. But the Allies summoned strength from the faith, belief, loyalty, and love of those who fell here. They built a new Europe together."

After the war, there was a reconciliation of enemies. The United States helped the rebuilding of Europe with the Marshall Plan. That aid led to NATO, "a great alliance that serves to this day as our shield for freedom, for prosperity, and for peace." But not all went well after the end of the war. Reagan now turns to a standard subject in his speeches from the 1950s forward, the need to oppose and eventually defeat communism, and particularly the Soviet Union. After the war, some countries saw an opportunity to increase their power and to subjugate others. "Some liberated countries were lost. The great sadness of this loss echoes down to our own time in the streets of Warsaw, Prague, and East Berlin. Soviet troops that came to the center of this continent did not leave when the peace came. They're still there, uninvited, unwanted, unyielding, almost 40 years after the war. Because of this, allied forces still stand on this continent." U.S. troops remain in Europe for one purpose—"to protect and defend democracy." The United States had not come to Normandy as a conqueror to gain territory: "The only territories we hold are memorials like this one and graveyards where our heroes rest."

Why does the United States continue to have troops in Europe? "We in America have learned bitter lessons from two World Wars: It is better to be here ready to protect the peace, than to take blind shelter across the sea, rushing to respond only after freedom is lost. We've learned that isolation never was and never will be an acceptable response to tyrannical governments with an expansionist intent." He asserts that the United States is ready for peace and willing to reconcile with the Soviet Union in order to lessen the potential of war, and then he speaks directly to the Soviets. He begins by remembering that Russia had suffered during World War II, losing twenty million citizens during the conflict. Their loss justifies the necessity of working to end war: "I tell you from my heart that we in the United States do not want war. We want to wipe from the face of the Earth the terrible weapons that man now has in his hands. And I tell you, we are ready to seize that beachhead. We look for some sign from the Soviet Union that they are willing to move forward, that they share our desire and love of peace, and that they will give up the ways of conflict."

Although he has hope that there will be peace in the future, Reagan takes consolation in the strength of the alliance between the United States and Europe. He speaks to Europeans and assures them that the United States will remain steadfast in its commitment to Europe: "We are bound today by what bound us 40 years ago, the same loyalties, traditions, and beliefs. We're bound by reality. The strength of America's allies is vital to the United States, and the American security guarantee is essential to the continued freedom of Europe's democracies. We were with you then; we are with you now. Your hopes are our hopes, and your destiny is our destiny."

He repeats the words of General Ridgway: "Here in this place where the West held together, let us make a vow to our dead. Let us show by our actions that we understand what they died for. Let our actions say to them the words for which Matthew Ridgway listened: 'I will not fail thee nor forsake thee.'"

He concludes the speech by calling for a commitment to maintaining freedom and hope in the world and asks everyone to remember the sacrifice of those who fought at Pointe du Hoc: "Strengthened by their courage, heartened by their valor, and borne by their memory, let us continue to stand for the ideals for which they lived and died."

After Reagan spoke, he "unveiled memorial plaques to the 2nd and 5th Ranger Battalions. Then, escorted by Phil Rivers, superintendent of the Normandy American Cemetery, the President and Mrs. Reagan proceeded to the interior of the observation bunker. On leaving the bunker, the President and Mrs. Reagan greeted each of the veterans."[57]

Reagan describes the situation before him on that day: "Sixty-two of the survivors were there for the anniversary; with gray hair and faces weathered by age and life's experiences, they might have been elderly businessmen, and I suppose some of them were; but these were the boys, some of them just starting to shave at the time, who had given so much, had been so brave at the dawn of the assault. On that windswept point for which so much blood had been spilled, I tried to recount the story of their bravery. I think it was an emotional experience for all of us."[58]

The speech was carefully written to not offend Chancellor Kohl and other German leaders, who not were invited to the ceremony, but it was also full of "tough, simmering, anti-Soviet Reaganesque language"—a continuation of the Reagan anti-Soviet rhetoric used in his European trips. Brinkley writes that the "words Noonan had written for him that afternoon were a distillation of his anti-communist thinking of almost four decades."[59] Wills proposes that the speech was an example of Reagan offering "the past as present,"[60] the same theme he would use a year later at Bergen-Belsen and Bitburg.

After leaving Pointe du Hoc, Reagan traveled to Omaha Beach, where he and President Mitterrand placed wreaths at a memorial to D-Day. The message he delivered, written by Tony Dolan, was emotional. Although it honored all soldiers who fought on that day, it used a typical Reagan tactic in which one individual is a metaphor for all soldiers. Reagan received a letter from "a California woman, Lisa Zanatta Henn, whose father, Private Peter Zanatta, had not yet been twenty when he waded out of a bobbing landing craft in the first wave of invaders at Omaha Beach on June 6, 1944."[61] Reagan used Private Zanatta's story as the basis for most of the speech. As a matter of fact, the entire speech can be seen as an extended story of this one American who fought in World War II and the reasons his efforts were not in vain.

The speech begins in a manner similar to the earlier one at Pointe du Hoc: "We stand today at a place of battle, one that 40 years ago saw and felt the worst of war. Men bled and died here for a few feet of—or inches of sand, as bullets and shellfire cut through their ranks. About them, General Omar Bradley later said, 'Every man who set foot on Omaha Beach that day was a hero.'" Reagan then recalls another war and another American president: "No speech can adequately portray their suffering, their sacrifice, their heroism. President Lincoln once reminded us that through their deeds, the dead of battle have spoken more eloquently for themselves than any of the living ever could. But we can only honor them by dedicating ourselves to the cause for which they gave a last full measure of devotion." He draws a lesson from their deaths: "Today we so rededicate ourselves to that cause. And at this place of honor, we're humbled by the realization of how much so many gave to the cause of freedom and to their fellow man."[62]

After honoring all who fought at Omaha Beach, Reagan makes a transition to Private Zanatta's story: "Some who survived the battle of June 6, 1944, are here today. Others who hoped to return never did." Reagan turns to the letter he received from Zanatta's daughter: "'Someday, Lis, I'll go back,' said Private Peter Robert Zanatta, of the 37th Engineer Combat Battalion, and first assault wave to hit Omaha Beach. 'I'll go back, and I'll see it again. I'll see the beach, the barricades, and the graves.'"

But Private Zanatta never made it back to Omaha Beach. His daughter wrote that the battle changed his life forever and that he vividly told the story of the day: "'He made me feel the fear of being in that boat waiting to land. I can smell the ocean and feel the seasickness. I can see the looks on his fellow soldiers' faces—the fear, the anguish, the uncertainty of what lay ahead. And when they landed, I can feel the strength and courage of the men who took those first steps through the tide to what must have surely looked like instant death.'"

Reagan again repeats the theme from Pointe du Hoc that soldiers like Private Zanatta came as liberators, not as conquerors. They fought as allies with members of the French resistance and soldiers of other nations. Reagan then shifts from the past to the present: "Today, in their memory, and for all who fought here, we celebrate the triumph of democracy. We reaffirm the unity of democratic peoples who fought a war and then joined the vanquished in a firm resolve to keep the peace." He proclaims what the United States learned from the war: "From a terrible war we learned that unity made us invincible; now, in peace, that same unity makes us secure. We sought to bring all freedom-loving nations together in a community dedicated to the defense and preservation of our sacred values. Our alliance, forged in the crucible of war, tempered and shaped by the realities of the postwar world, has succeeded. In Europe, the threat has been contained, the peace has been kept." He again points out that politicians, citizens, and soldiers are gathered "as a tribute to what was achieved here 40 years ago. This land is secure. We are free. These things are worth fighting and dying for." As at Pointe du Hoc, Reagan commemorates the achievements of 1944 but reminds his audience that they must be vigilant in 1984 because there are enemies who would like to destroy the freedom that was so difficult to achieve forty years earlier.

In his conclusion he returns to the letter from Private Zanatta's daughter. Her father had died eight years earlier from cancer, and she made a promise to him that she would return to Normandy in his place: "'I'm going there, Dad, and I'll see the beaches and the barricades and the monuments. I'll see the graves, and I'll put flowers there just like you wanted to do. I'll feel all the things you made me feel through your stories and your eyes. I'll never forget what you went through, Dad, nor will I let anyone else forget. And, Dad, I'll always be proud.'"

Reagan invited Zanatta's daughter to attend the ceremony and read from her letter, which apparently had a considerable effect on him. Reagan later wrote that, "after a few minutes, it was all but impossible to go on. My voice began to crack. But I managed to get through it and was glad when I reached the end."[63]

Lisa Zanatta Henn was present to hear the speech's moving conclusion: "Through the words of his loving daughter, who is here with us today, a D-day veteran has shown us the meaning of this day far better than any President can. It is enough for us to say about Private Zanatta and all the men of honor and courage who fought beside him four decades ago: We will always remember. We will always be proud. We will always be prepared, so we may always be free."

Reagan staffer Michael Deaver adds an interesting note to the events: "The president, incidentally, personally paid her way to Normandy."[64] He also kept in contact with her for years after the speech and used her father as an image in several speeches after this one, including his farewell address. As Brinkley says, "The story of Private First Class Peter Robert Zanatta would get recycled in other high-profile Reagan speeches to come."[65]

The two speeches that commemorated the fortieth anniversary of D-Day were prime examples of successful ceremonial oratory. They show that Reagan could use story and emotion in striking visual setting. Their success should also make it clear that well-written speeches were crucial in the Reagan White House. Because Reagan was judged by the quality of his speeches, a great deal of pressure was placed on speechwriters to produce effective messages.

Robinson did admit a problem in writing Reagan's speeches, especially those to be delivered in foreign countries: Reagan seems to have been unsure "about the impact his speeches might have outside the United States."[66] This is interesting, since some of Reagan's most effective speeches were delivered during his travels abroad. The speeches at Pointe du Hoc and Omaha Beach are examples of Reagan at his best. He delivered well-written, emotional speeches in settings that were visually striking. Perhaps they were successful because Reagan was still speaking to an American audience even though the speeches were delivered in France.

CHAPTER 3

Events Leading to Speeches
at Bergen-Belsen and Bitburg

After the positive reception of the speeches at Pointe du Hoc and Omaha Beach in 1984, Reagan seemed more secure in ceremonial speaking situations in Europe. Within a year he returned to Europe for ceremonies celebrating the fortieth anniversary of the end of World War II in Europe, but his speeches on that trip were far less successful. The controversy surrounding this trip exposed weaknesses in the White House staff in Reagan's second administration and some of Reagan's own personality flaws, particularly his stubbornness and unwillingness to alter his itinerary and message even when changing that message might have been wise.

The Controversy over Reagan's Visit

On November 30, 1984, Reagan met with Chancellor Helmut Kohl of West Germany in Washington, D.C. At the conclusion of the visit, Reagan accepted an invitation to lay a wreath at a German military cemetery. The White House sent Michael Deaver to Germany in February 1985 to select a site for the ceremony. Deaver was a public relations expert who had found locations for many of Reagan's most successful speeches. "I was charged with handling the advance work and planning for the entire trip. Along with our diplomatic team in Bonn, we selected what I thought was the perfect site to lay a wreath to remember the German war dead. The cemetery I reviewed was ideal, beautifully coated with a long winter's snowfall."[1] The cemetery in Bitburg, called the Kolmeshohe cemetery, was close to a U.S. military base: "After thirty-three years of fraternization and intermarriage, the area was about as Americanized as any in the Federal Republic. Both Reagan and Kohl—who as a boy in 1945 had been rescued from near starvation by U.S. food trucks—would feel comfortable there."[2] The spot seemed to be ideal, but there were problems hidden beneath the snow. Deaver claimed that he did not do his usual thorough job because he was in the process of leaving government and starting his own public relations firm.

After making the selection, Deaver instructed the staff at the U.S. embassy in West Germany to make sure there were no hidden embarrassments in the cemetery. He received assurances from German chief of protocol Werner von der Schulenberg that "no war criminals" were buried there. Unfortunately, forty-nine Waffen SS soldiers were buried there. Deaver's successor, William Henkel, asked about potential problems in a follow-up trip in March but was given no further information that would raise concerns. The trip itinerary was approved by the president and his staff in March.

The plans for the trip were announced by White House spokesperson Larry Speakes in Santa Barbara on April 11. At the press conference, Speakes was asked the identity of the soldiers buried in Bitburg. There had been newspaper reports that the cemetery contained only graves of German soldiers. Speakes did not know the answer but promised to investigate the situation and report his findings to the press. Even though stories about Reagan's proposed trip did not contain information about the SS soldiers, they caused a furor among veterans of World War II and their families because they believed that only German soldiers would be honored during Reagan's trip.[3]

The announcement also offended many Jewish individuals because April 11 came at the height of Passover. Elie Wiesel, the Nobel Prize–winning author, expressed Jewish frustration: The timing of the announcement was "so crassly offensive to the feelings of Jews. . . . Rarely have I known such outrage."[4] Wiesel and others thought the announcement at such an important time was the result of incompetent staff work and did not reflect the president's personal views. Reagan was vacationing at his ranch in the hills above Santa Barbara at the time.

The furor only increased when the news about the graves of the Waffen SS soldiers broke during the weekend of April 13–14. The Waffen SS, or Schutzstaffel, was the combat arm of Hitler's elite guard and for many Americans represented the most heinous criminals of the Third Reich. The Nuremberg war crimes tribunal had judged the SS guilty of abominations, including exterminating Jews and killing prisoners of war.[5] One of the soldiers was SS Sgt. Otto Franz Begel, who had earned the German Cross for killing ten Americans in one day, on a day when seventy or more captured Americans were executed and buried in a shallow mass grave.[6] American Jews and veterans continued to be frustrated that Reagan did not plan to visit a concentration camp or U.S. military cemetery. One Reagan aide illustrated the extent of the anger: "I never thought I'd see the day when Ronald Reagan could get the American Legion angry with him, by God, we've done it."[7]

From the middle of April until the date of the speeches on May 5, Reagan was under constant attack. He and his staff undertook a concerted persuasive campaign to limit the damage caused by the proposed itinerary. Rhetorical critic Kathryn M. Olson observes that this campaign on Reagan's part involved the use of definition and redefinition; "defining and redefining events and situations to put one's responses to them in the best possible light abound in practice, especially in political rhetoric." Reagan initially "defined his trip as an act designed to end formally an era of U.S.–West German relations characterized by American anger and recriminations over World War II and to usher in an era of newly strengthened ties with West Germany." Once the opposition arose, Reagan tried to redefine the trip, but his redefinitions "consistently reasserted a particular perspective or worldview, one that was unacceptable to his Jewish opponents, instead of signaling a change of perspective."[8]

Reagan stubbornly refused to change his position. Those who worked with him or knew him well commented that, once he made a decision, it was virtually impossible to get him to modify his stance, especially when the decision involved someone he viewed as a friend, like Chancellor Kohl. That trait was obvious throughout the controversy and may have prevented him from calming the criticism of at least some of his opponents.

Communication scholar Robert V. Friedenberg considers Reagan's rhetoric leading up to his visits to Bergen-Belsen and Bitburg a series of apologies that were often delivered in situations where others were in control, such as press conferences during which reporters selected the questions asked and subjects to be discussed. Friedenberg notes that Reagan's discourse included the tactic of denying "intent, arguing that a statement or action had been misunderstood." He also argues that Reagan used a strategy of identifying with "something viewed favorably by the audience in order to 'bolster' his image." His journey to Bergen-Belsen was viewed positively by many members of his audience, so he linked that event with his visit to Bitburg in an attempt to improve his image. Unfortunately, Friedenberg argues, Reagan made errors in his apologies that weakened his appeals—though the carefully crafted speeches at Bergen-Belsen and Bitburg later allowed him to apologize effectively.[9]

Deaver outlines the tremendous pressure Reagan faced during the controversy: "I don't think I saw Reagan under more intense pressure than during the Bitburg crisis. My life became a living hell, so I can only imagine what Ronald Reagan was going through."[10] Because of the intensity of emotions during the controversy, many people, including Nancy Reagan, wanted the president to cancel the trip, but he refused: "I told her that once I'd accepted the invitation, I could not embarrass Helmut Kohl by canceling the visit. But that wasn't the only reason I refused to cancel."[11] Reagan often became more stubborn "when he was asked to back away from a personal commitment for political reasons," and it was obvious that canceling the trip could only occur because of political pressure.[12] Reagan describes the issue in his diary: "All of this was portrayed as being willing to honor former Nazis but trying to forget the Holocaust. Helmut [Kohl] had in mind observing the end of World War II anniversary as the end of hatred and the beginning of friendship and peace that has lasted 40 years. I have repeatedly said we must never forget the Holocaust and remember it so it will never happen again. But some of our Jewish friends are now on the warpath. There is no way I'll back down and run for cover."[13]

His second reason for not canceling the trip was more controversial: "I didn't think it was right to keep on punishing every German for the Holocaust, including generations not yet born in the time of Hitler. I don't think all Germans deserve to bear the stigma for everything he [Hitler] did." Rather, Reagan believed that West Germany should be praised for its attempts to educate its citizens about the horror of the Holocaust: "The modern German government has attempted to come to grips with the horrors of Hitler's monstrous crimes by keeping memories of them alive; it has turned former concentration camps into museums of death containing the most horrifying pictures you have ever seen, and encouraged German schoolchildren to visit the museums and look at the pictures."[14]

Historian Garry Wills claims that Reagan wanted to speak from the cemetery because of the visual imagery: "One answer is that the Bitburg cemetery is photogenic, and Reagan is good at tributes to dead soldiers."[15] The D-Day commemoratives in 1984 were prime examples of such photogenic settings and emotional speeches honoring living and dead soldiers, and Deaver was a master of choosing sites that placed Reagan in visually striking settings where he could best use his abilities as an orator: "If I am qualified as an expert on anything, it was said to be the staging of a media event; blending the gifts of Ronald Reagan with the proper pageantry."[16] But Deaver was distracted in the period before the trip to Germany. Aside from leaving the White House and thinking a great deal about the public relations firm he was starting, he also was not physically well, having just recovered from a kidney ailment complicated by an allergic reaction.[17] It was later disclosed that Deaver had a serious drinking problem.

Deaver knew that Reagan was a more effective speaker in some situations than others, and it was his job to place him in settings that would emphasize his strengths, not his weaknesses. He had learned to keep

Reagan out of certain types of highly emotional situations: "I had the additional factor of Ronald Reagan's nature. He was not at ease with, not eager to confront, scenes of unrelenting depression. He was at his best when he could touch the nostalgia, the longing in each of us for a more romantic time. You put him near a flag, around uniforms, or in sight of a parade, and he could lift anyone's spirit." Deaver did not want Reagan to visit a concentration camp. "I knew Reagan's emotions would betray him in such a setting. . . . Reagan simply could not perform in certain environments. During a stop at a veteran's home in 1980, he was unable to complete his prepared text before losing his composure. He saw too many ghosts in the eyes of the ailing men in front of him."[18]

In spite of his reservations, Deaver eventually proposed the addition of a visit to a concentration camp: "I had decided to add a side trip to a concentration camp after all, the one at Bergen-Belsen. The move exposed us to charges of flip-flopping, and reeked of politics, but our objective now was to balance Bitburg, not reject it."[19] The decision would mean a definite change in plans that the White House had to explain without admitting that the decision was made for political reasons.

Reagan would agree to the addition of a trip to a concentration camp only if he received a formal invitation from Kohl to visit an acceptable site. That stipulation provided Reagan some coverage when he was questioned about changing his mind concerning such a visit. After discussions with Kohl, the itinerary was altered and a trip to the concentration camp site was added. Reagan wrote in his diary, "Helmut is making it official. He'll invite me to visit the camp as well as the cemetery. I can accept both now that it's official."[20] Because of Kohl's invitation, Reagan could attempt to redefine the situation and say that the idea for the schedule change came from the German government, not the United States. Later the German government would change the itinerary from Dachau to Bergen-Belsen. Many critics in the United States were not placated by the addition.

Bergen-Belsen was established in 1940. Until 1943 it was a prisoner-of-war camp for French, Belgian, and Russian soldiers. In 1943 a "residence camp" was formed to house Jewish prisoners under the pretext that they would be exchanged for German prisoners. Few of the detainees were ever exchanged. In December 1944, Bergen-Belsen was designated a concentration camp. It became a collection camp for Jewish prisoners who were moved from other camps as the Allies advanced into Germany. By April 1945 the camp population had risen from 4,000 inmates to more than 60,000. As many as 35,000 people died because of overcrowding, poor sanitary conditions, and a lack of food and shelter that led to a typhus epidemic. The camp was liberated on April 15, 1945, by British soldiers. The British evacuated the camp and then burned it to prevent the spread of typhus.[21]

Deaver and Henkel left for Germany on April 15 to survey potential concentration camp sites, leaving Donald Regan, the new White House chief of staff, in control of the situation at home. Unfortunately, the chief of staff was angry with Jewish leaders because of their questioning of the president and ended up offending them further. A group of Jewish leaders, including Elie Wiesel, had been invited to the White House on April 16 to discuss alternatives to the Bitburg visit. The invitation was not sincere because Regan was unwilling to consider any changes. Even before the meeting convened, he had prepared a statement that the president would deliver to a conference on religious liberty on the same day as the meeting with Jewish leaders. Reagan was to announce that he was visiting Germany "to commemorate not simply the military victory of forty years ago but the liberation of Europe, the rebirth of German freedom and the reconciliation of two countries." He would begin the process of redefining the situation by stating that he would go to a concentration camp, a stop not included in his original itinerary, because "of a mistaken impression that such a visit was outside the official agenda."[22]

During the meeting with Regan, Jewish leaders discovered the president's actions and left the White House in anger. Reagan's speech to participants at the conference on religious liberty was being delivered at the same time the Jewish leaders were leaving. He apparently was not aware of the unsuccessful gathering.

At the conference, Reagan delivers his prepared text outlining the growth of religious freedom throughout the world and then adds at the end, "Let me turn to an issue, if I could for just a moment, that has provoked a storm of controversy: my decision to visit the war cemetery at Bitburg and my decision, on the state visit to Germany, not to visit the site of the concentration camp at Dachau."[23] Reagan reiterates his assertion that his trip's goal is "to commemorate not simply the military victory of 40 years ago but the liberation of Europe, the rebirth of German freedom, and the reconciliation of our two countries." He states that his purpose is "not to reemphasize the crimes of the Third Reich" but to celebrate the "tremendous accomplishments of the German people in 40 years of liberty, freedom, democracy, and peace" as well as "cement the 40 years of friendship between a free Germany and the United States, between the German people and the American people."

Reagan now turns to his attempt to redefine the situation, stating that his reason for not planning to visit Dachau (or any other concentration camp), "one of the sites of the great moral obscenity of that era," is based on his "mistaken impression that such a visit was outside the official agenda." He claims that Chancellor Kohl had made clear to him that the visit is part of the official agenda and so he has accepted. "My staff is in Germany exploring a site that will fit into our schedule there." He concludes with words he would repeat numerous times in the coming days: "For years I've said it, and I'll say it again today, and I will say it again on that occasion: We must never forget the Holocaust, nor should we ever permit such an atrocity to happen again. Never again."

Reagan's lack of supervision of his staff may have been at fault throughout the controversy. Bob Schieffer and Gary Paul Gates detail the importance of effective staff work in times of crisis: "If God is found in the details, so too are the demons on occasion, and Bitburg was one of those occasions. Poor staff work by Reagan's usually reliable advancemen, missteps by the West German government, and a series of errors by Reagan himself resulted in the most embarrassing episode—up to that point—in Reagan's presidency. What had been planned as a quick trip to Bitburg became 'the Bitburg mess.'"[24]

This mess occurred during a time of dramatic change in the Reagan White House staff. In his first term Reagan had been served by an extremely loyal and effective staff. Unfortunately, many of those individuals had left the White House. Donald Regan replaced James Baker as the White House chief of staff. Though Regan had a long history as an administrator in the private sector and in government, he did not have Baker's ability to manage the complex political situations facing the president and his staff. When he came to the White House, Regan brought a loyal group of subordinates who were labeled "the mice" by other members of the staff because of the negative effect they had on the workings of the White House. The mice were highly loyal to Regan but were inexperienced in the kind of politics necessary to keep the White House functioning. Staffer Peggy Noonan and others believed that they so restricted access to the president that there simply were not enough people with input into decisions and therefore available to manage crises. "But what he [Regan] and the other mice did was they created a hierarchical bottleneck—and all movement stopped. And so Bitburg came along, and it paralyzed the entire process because it totally consumed the few people who could do anything. They didn't create order—they created paralysis."[25]

On April 18, fifty-three senators announced their opposition to the Bitburg visit. On that same day, Reagan held a question-and-answer session with a group of regional editors and broadcasters.[26] During that session he was asked about the senators' concerns and whether he and his staff anticipated negative political ramifications when they set their itinerary for the trip. Reagan's responses only made the situation worse. He began by stating that he should have listened to the press earlier, a comment that drew laughter from those present, and then observed that part of the problem was that he had not explained clearly why he would not visit a concentration camp. He provided details about Kohl and Mitterand's trip to a World War I cemetery at Verdun and how that journey helped heal wounds between those long-time adversaries. Kohl had recommended that Reagan visit a cemetery, and the one at Bitburg was chosen: "We have a base there and . . . I'm going there and go to church with them and have lunch with them. And the Kohls will be with us, also." He then repeated the explanation that he had rejected a stop at a concentration camp because he thought the invitation was from a private citizen, not from the government: "And I thought there was not the way that I, as the guest of the government at that point could on my own take off and go someplace and then, run the risk of appearing as if I was trying to say to the Germans, 'Look what you did,' and all of this when most of the people in German today weren't alive or were very small children when this was happening." He recalled that foreign leaders from Germany, Japan, and Italy had traveled to Arlington Cemetery near Washington, D.C., when they visited the United States; such visits by heads of government were common.

Reagan also discussed the discovery of the existence of the SS graves, which he emphasized were a small minority of the graves in the cemetery. He used a line that he would repeat throughout the controversy, claiming that most of those buried in Bitburg were young victims of the Nazis: "The average age is about 18. These were youngsters who were conscripted, forced into military service in the closing days of the Third Reich when they were short of manpower." He believed that a visit to the cemetery was as a way of announcing, "Let's resolve, in their presence, as well as in the presence of our own troops, that this must never happen again." He explained that he had received a cable from Kohl assuring him that a trip to a concentration camp was part of the official itinerary, so he agreed to visit one to "make it clear that we're determined the Holocaust must never take place again."

At this point he was interrupted and asked if his statement meant that he was still going to Bitburg. He responded that it would look as though he had "caved in in the face of some unfavorable attention" if he did not go to the cemetery. He then got himself further in trouble by saying that there was nothing wrong with visiting the cemetery, because "those young men are victims of Nazism also, even though they were fighting in the German uniform, drafted into service to carry out the hateful wishes of the Nazis. They were victims, just as surely as the victims in the concentration camps." That line offended Jewish leaders, who did not accept that German soldiers and prisoners in concentration camps were equally victims of Nazism. In their view, many soldiers willingly fought for Nazi beliefs and supported actions such as putting millions of people in concentration camps. Although the line was offensive to many, it was one that Reagan used in other settings, and it appeared in the Bitburg speech.

On April 19, in a dramatic event that had been scheduled long before the controversy, the president honored Elie Wiesel, a Jewish writer and survivor of the Holocaust, and other Jewish leaders were invited to the White House for the Jewish Heritage Week ceremony. At that ceremony Reagan presented Wiesel with the Congressional Gold Medal. The events of the day were stunning and illustrate the deep division between Reagan and many Jews caused by his Bitburg plans.

Reagan's speech to the assembled audience outlines the accomplishments of Jewish people.[27] He comments that Jews have just finished celebrating Passover and then turns his attention to the Holocaust. He states that Jewish people swore an oath at the end of World War II, "Never again," and the United States has made the same pledge—"And we've kept it. We kept it when we supported the establishment of the state of Israel, the refuge that the Jewish people lacked during the Holocaust, the dream of generations, the sure sign of God's hand in history." He says that the United States had also helped Ethiopian Jews and Soviet Jews and established the Holocaust Memorial Commission and laid a cornerstone for its museum. He praises the survivors of the concentration camps and others for helping Americans remember the events of the past and notes that Americans are praying for a better world in the future. He then reiterates one of the standard appeals used throughout the controversy: "Today, there is a spirit of reconciliation between the peoples of the allied nations and the people of Germany and even between the soldiers who fought each other on the battlefields of Europe. That spirit must grow and be strengthened." He goes on to praise Wiesel for his many accomplishments and presents him the medal. Reagan could not have anticipated what happened next.

Wiesel had seriously considered declining the award to show his concern about the visit to Bitburg, but he finally agreed to the honor because it had been voted by members of Congress.[28] He used the ceremony to deliver the kind of powerful attack that was seldom heard in the White House or in speeches given by individuals accepting honors on other occasions. He begins by thanking the president and then quickly steps into the fray about Bitburg: "Mr. President, speaking of reconciliation, I was very pleased that we met before so a stage of reconciliation has been set in motion between us. But then we were never on two sides: we were on the same side. We were always on the side of justice, always on the side of memory, against the SS, and against what they represent." He explains that the medal is not his but belongs to those who remember the actions of the SS and those who read his writings in which he calls for honesty between individuals. He details his own life in the concentration camps during World War II and the lives of others who had opposed Nazis. He expresses his thanks to the U.S. military in World War II and for the leadership of the United States in the world. He thanks the president for being a friend of the Jewish people: "We have met four or five times, and each time I came away enriched, for I know of your commitment to humanity." He states that he believes that Reagan was not aware of the existence of the SS graves at Bitburg and then makes a powerful plea: "May I, Mr. President, if it's possible at all, implore you to do something else, to find a way, to find another way, another site. That place, Mr. President, is not your place. Your place is with the victims of the SS." He recognizes that there are political reasons for going to Bitburg, but the issue "is not politics but good and evil. And we must never confuse them, for I have seen the SS at work, and I have seen their victims." He concludes by saying that he understood that Reagan is seeking reconciliation and that he does not believe in collective guilt for all Germans, only for those who were responsible for the deaths of millions in World War II. He believes that all people must work together to "bring peace and understanding to a tormented world that, as you know, is still awaiting redemption."[29]

Reagan's biographer, Edmund Morris, believes that "it was the first time Reagan had ever been lectured in front of the American people. His eyes flicked sideways, and he blinked with disbelief. George Bush, who less than an hour before had been obsequiously praising the President for standing by Kohl, ran nervous fingers over his razor burn."[30] Schieffer and Gates echo Morris's words: "It was a stunning moment.

Almost never is an American President lectured in public, but that was precisely what was happening. Except for Wiesel's voice no sound could be heard in the room."[31]

After the meeting, Reagan was angry. He announced, "The final word has been spoken as far as I'm concerned. I think it is morally right to do what I'm doing, and I'm not going to change my mind about that." He then proclaimed that "all of those in the cemetery have long met the Supreme Judge of right and wrong, and whatever punishment or justice as was needed has been rendered by One who is above us all."[32] He used that theme throughout the controversy and it appeared in his speech at Bitburg. In his autobiography, Reagan was more positive in his description of the events of the day: "I explained the situation to them and made some gains even if later Elie in his prepared remarks implored me not to visit the cemetery. We've invited Elie to accompany me on the trip. He's said yes except that he won't be present at the cemetery."[33]

Reagan faced a difficult situation in talking about concentration camps. On more than one occasion he had publicly proclaimed that he visited the concentration camps at the end of World War II, something that was impossible because he did not leave the United States during the war. Wills claims that Reagan's staff did not want information about Reagan's past statements being made public. Cannon believes that Reagan convinced himself that he actually visited locations such as Normandy and the concentration camps during World War II because he vividly remembered movies about those places, so "he had already been there in his mind." Cannon quotes Reagan on his propensity to remember movies so vividly that became real life to him: "Maybe I had seen too many war movies, the heroics of which I sometimes confused with real life." Cannon carefully documents two separate incidents in which Reagan told Jewish leaders that he was so concerned about the plight of the Jews because he had "served as a Signal Corps photographer who had filmed the horrors of the Nazi death camps." Cannon knew that this claim was impossible.[34]

On other occasions, Reagan stated that during World War II he had been one of the first to view raw footage of the liberation of Buchenwald and that he had kept some of that film to show people who did not believe the Holocaust happened. "He could not forget and never would."[35] He said that he had seen secret movies about the camps, but Cannon counters that these secret movies had been shown in American theaters as early as April 1945.[36]

Reagan often spoke of being deeply affected by the films: "During the final months of the war, we began receiving secret Signal Corps films showing the liberation of Hitler's death camps and they engraved images on my mind that will be there forever." He described images from the films: "There were many other ghastly images: Camp inmates so gaunt and emaciated you wonder how they could possibly be alive; ditches filled with bodies being bulldozed into the earth; footage of German families brought from nearby villages to see for themselves the unspeakable inhumanity of their countrymen."[37]

Reagan said that he kept a copy of the films just in case people needed to be reminded of Hitler's terrible acts. Later he showed the films to his children and to individuals who expressed doubts that the camps had existed. During the events surrounding Bitburg he could point to his actions to illustrate his concern that the events of World War II never be forgotten.[38] Deaver explains that Reagan had seen pictures of concentration camps in footage sent home by the Signal Corps: "He saw this nightmare on film, not in person. That did not mean he saw it less."[39] Cannon supports Deaver's views: "What must be said here is that Reagan was not insensitive to the Holocaust. He shared the views of Jews and many others that the Holocaust must be remembered so it can never happen again. His imagined accounts of having filmed the liberation of the death camps showed not only his difficulty in distinguishing actual from cinematic experience but the deep impression the Holocaust had made upon him."[40]

The reaction to the Wiesel event and other news about Bitburg was significant for the press: "When a bushfire like Bitburg flares after a long news drought, the American press becomes pyromaniacal." Morris describes the press as actively fanning the flames for the next month.[41]

Reagan continued to receive criticism for his decision to visit the cemetery. Individuals from whom he usually received support, like Sen. Robert Dole of Kansas, questioned Reagan's decision. Dole's criticism led to an interesting exchange between Reagan and a reporter on April 25. On that date Reagan delivered a speech at the White House honoring youth volunteers. At the conclusion of the speech he received a plaque honoring him for his support of young people. After the presentation a reporter asked, "Mr. President, Senator Dole says your visit to Bitburg will be less than appropriate, sir. Are you considering changing your plans?" Reagan's response showed that he had no such plan: "I'm just considering putting this [the plaque] on my desk."[42]

On that same day, he participated in a lengthy interview with foreign journalists.[43] After a discussion that covered a wide range of topics, the issue of his visit was raised by a German reporter: "We Germans hope your heart is not too heavy after all these misunderstandings regarding your visit." The reporter then asked Reagan what message he wished to send to the German people. Reagan's response was typical of what he had been saying throughout the controversy: "The message that I would have for them, and particularly in this anniversary situation that is coming up, is one of recognition that for 40 years we have been friends. The summit meeting consists of the heads of state of countries that were 40 years ago bitter enemies. We're friends; we have been at peace. I would extend my own admiration for the democracy that the people of Germany have created in these 40 years, for their dedication to democratic ideals, and that would observe this particular time as one of recognition of the reconciliation that has taken place between one-time enemies and which we are more than reconciled—we have become close friends and allies."

The reporter then stated, "You will not comment on Bitburg, I guess." Reagan responded, "No, no. I am going to be a guest of your government, I'm looking forward to the entire trip." The reported responded, "The German people would like to welcome you very much."

The situation was more confrontational on April 29 when Reagan met with another group of foreign journalists.[44] The first question in the press conference focuses on Bitburg and in some ways summarizes the objections Reagan's critics made to the trip: "The controversy over your intended Bitburg cemetery visit is sharpening, and it overshadows the economic summit, and it spoils your ideas of reconciliation. The [members of] Congress urge you not to go. The veterans urge you not to go. And the Holocaust victims urge you not to go. And the majority of the American people are against this visit. Mr. President, how does this turmoil of emotions affect you personally and politically and has the final word been spoken on Bitburg?" Reagan replies in his now typical fashion: "The final word has been spoken as far as I am concerned. I think it is morally right to do what I'm doing, and I'm not going to change my mind about that." This is another example of Reagan consistently maintaining that his actions are morally right throughout the controversy, and as a secular preacher morality was a central issue in Reagan's life.

He continues his answer by disagreeing that the majority of Americans oppose the visit and then takes a slap at the press: "I think they've gotten a hold of something, and, like a dog worrying a bone, they're going to keep chewing on it." He reiterates his view that the visit is a celebration of forty years of friendship in which old enemies can become friends and again states that events like the Holocaust must never occur again. He concludes, "And if that is what we can bring out of these observances and the trip that has been planned, then I think everything we're doing is worthwhile."

Reagan is asked if mistakes by planners in Washington, D.C., and Bonn led to the crisis. He attempts to redefine the issue by responding with his previously stated position that much of the problem is the result of his not thoroughly answering a question about a possible visit to a concentration camp. He says that when the invitation for the visit was extended, he and Kohl agreed that it should not be a celebration "when we should be out shooting off fireworks and celebrating a victory or commiserating a victory or a defeat." He now uses a theme that would appear again in his speech at Bitburg: Unlike other wars that "planted the seeds of the next war and left hatreds that grew and grew until there would be another war," World War II led to peace and friendship among old enemies. He continues his redefinition by repeating that he had misinterpreted the invitation for a visit to a concentration camp and agreed to such a visit once he knew it was part of the official agenda.

The final questioner asks if he is aware that some of the SS troops buried in Bitburg may have participated in a massacre in the French village of Oradour in which 642 people died. Reagan does not respond directly to the question. Rather, he falls back on statements he had used previously: "I know all the bad things that happened in that war. I was in uniform for 4 years myself. And again, all of those—you're asking with reference to people who are in the cemetery, who are buried there. Well, I've said to some of my friends about that, all of those in that cemetery have long since met the supreme judge of right and wrong. And whatever punishment or justice was needed has been rendered by one who is above us all." He reiterates that he is not going to Europe to honor anyone: "It's going there simply to, in that surrounding, more visibly bring to the people an awareness of the great reconciliation that has take place, and, as I've said before—too many times, I guess—the need to remember in the sense of being pledged to never letting it happen again."

Reagan continued to use such lines, but the press and other critics would not stop questioning the decision. At one point his resolve seemed to weaken, and there was consideration of canceling the trip, but Reagan reaffirmed his plans after a telephone conversation with Kohl.

As the controversy continued, the White House attempted to counter criticism with carefully crafted responses by the president in his public appearances, and the gist of those responses appeared in speeches delivered during the trip. For example, seven answers were provided for the president to respond to the hypothetical question, "Why Going to Bitburg?"[45] One of the prepared comments provided a justification for the president's acceptance of Chancellor Kohl's invitation: "Included in that invitation was the stop at Bitburg that has aroused so many bitter memories of the Holocaust. Of course we should never, can never, forget such a tragedy. Nor should we ever permit it to happen again. But it was not to ignore the past but, on the contrary, to stress how far we have come—and from where—that I have made the decision to go to Bitburg and that I will visit also the former concentration camp at Bergen-Belsen."

Another answer acknowledged the significant political implications the trip carried: "Chancellor Kohl has stressed to us his judgment that a change in the program now would have grave and adverse consequences not only in terms of domestic politics in the Federal Republic but for the larger interests of German-American relations." Another response reflected Reagan's determination to follow his initial decision: "Unless that judgment changes, I intend to hold to the plans we have announced."

Comments were also provided for staff members when they were asked questions about the visit to the concentration camp and the cemetery. The prepared answers were consistent with the comments the president was making in public. They pointed to the meeting at Verdun between Kohl and Mitterand the previous year, contained an affirmation that the horrible events of World War II should never occur again, and focused on the "reconciliation and friendship which have made post-war Germany and the U.S. the strongest of allies." The response to the problem of the SS graves contained an implied admission of the failure of Reagan's staff and combined that admission with a theme that appeared in the speech at Bitburg: "At the time the President decided to go to Bitburg, it was not known that any SS soldiers were buried at Bitburg. As it turns out, there are some 40–50 SS graves—out of 2,000 in all. Most of those buried were very young, forced into service in the closing days of the Third Reich." The issue of young people who died during World War II would become a major theme in the speeches at Bergen-Belsen and Bitburg.

Responses to questions concerning leaving the trip plans unchanged in spite of the outcry by Jewish leaders, Congress, and concerned individuals again focused on the president's desire to commemorate not "the military victory of 40 years ago but the liberation of Europe, the beginning of peace, the rebirth of German freedom and the reconciliation of our two countries." One answer referred to the events of the previous year: "As with Verdun, the cemetery stands as a solemn testament to the tragedy and horror of the war between our two peoples." A final response for a speaker "if pressed" admitted to political considerations: "It is true that considerations of security (communications, logistics, etc.) as well as proximity (Bitburg is in Chancellor Kohl's home constituency, Rhineland-Palatinate) entered into the decision."

There are two sets of prepared responses that attempted to redefine the reason for Reagan's decision to go to a concentration camp after first announcing that he would not undertake such a journey. The first repeated Reagan's statement that he did not understand that the visit was included in Chancellor Kohl's official invitation. The second stated that Reagan did not want to impose "a further sense of guilt" on the Germans living today who did not participate in the war, that the decision was not an attempt to "balance" or "trade-off" the visits, and that the visit did not affect his view that the Holocaust must never happen again. There was an attempt to differentiate the reasons for stopping at two different locations: "The two stops are being made on their own independent merits: Bergen-Belsen to commemorate the Holocaust—to honor the victims of the Nazi outrage; Bitburg to demonstrate 40 years of peace in Europe, the tragedy and horror of war, and the mood of reconciliation between our two countries."

Reagan also attempted to justify his actions through responses to letters and other forms of personal communication. For example, he received a letter dated March 30, 1985, from Jesse A. Zeeman. At the top of the letter, which is in the Reagan Library, the word "Sample" is written, indicating that this was typical of the letters received by the White House during the controversy.[46] The president wrote on the letter, "Can we get address? RR." Reagan wanted the address so he could respond personally to Zeeman.

Zeeman stated his outrage that the president was not visiting a concentration camp during his trip: "There are many Germans alive who participated in that infamous pogrom, the abuse and slaughter of six million Jews is a part of German's heritage and should not be allowed to be forgotten lest it happen again." Reagan's carefully worded response, dated April 17, 1985, could serve as a model for answers to similar letter writers on the same subject. In his note Reagan blames much of the turmoil on the press: "Let me say in my own defense that the media presentation of this whole episode is a gross distortion of fact. I'll try to put the matter in proper perspective." He uses his standard tactic of trying to redefine the issues by stating that he thought the original invitation to visit a concentration camp came from a political figure in Germany and not the chancellor. Once he discovered that the visit to a concentration camp was part of the original invitation, he changed his itinerary. He then reiterates his view of the Holocaust: "Mr. Zeeman, my feelings about the Holocaust can be summed up in the words I've used a hundred times; 'we must never forget and it must never happen again.' Since I've been President we have regularly hosted gatherings in the East Room of survivors of the Holocaust. I'm more pleased than I can say that the visit to a concentration camp will be a part of the official program."

Marshall Breger served as special assistant to the president for public liaison. In that position he acted as the liaison between the White House and the Jewish community, so he was prominent in dealings with Reagan's critics. Breger tried to convince Reagan and his advisors to take specific actions to reduce the concerns of the Jewish community. One of his constant themes was a proposal that the Kaddish be said at the ceremony at Bergen-Belsen. On April 25 he wrote a memo to William Henkel strongly proposing that action: "It is absolutely necessary that the visit to Bergen-Belsen include a recitation of the *Kaddish,* the Jewish memorial prayer for the dead. I recognize that the service is non-denominational, but note that at the German Bergen-Belsen commemoration last week the *Kaddish* was said."[47]

On the same day, Breger wrote a memo to presidential advisor Ed Rollins outlining several actions he thought were crucial for the president to take at Bitburg: "The key to salvaging the President's trip to Germany is not what happens at Bergen-Belsen, but what happens at Bitburg.[48] We could do a terrific job of reconciliation at the concentration camp and flop for history if the Bitburg ceremony goes wrong." He proposed several points for consideration:

1. The president should distinguish between the German soldiers who "as tragedies of war, died in battle and the Waffen S.S."
2. The president should not enter the cemetery but rather speak outside the gate. Mitterand and Kohl did not enter the cem-

etery at Verdun, so the "President need not actually enter the cemetery to pay his respects to those worthy of respect."

3. If the president does enter the cemetery, he should not lay a wreath.

4. The SS graves "should be cordoned off" and the "President should not go near them."

5. There should be an attempt to see if there are any World War I graves at the cemetery. If there are, the president should acknowledge them "instead of World War II graves" because World War I "is not today remembered as a struggle between good and evil."

6. "The President's motorcade should stop briefly at the Jewish cemetery at Bitburg."

Breger argued that these or similar decisions should be announced quickly and that it was crucial that it be made very clear that the president was not going to honor the SS because this "will allow us to draw off some of the venom from the poison to recent days." Breger also expressed concern about individuals who would be demonstrating outside the cemetery. He suggested that the president consider addressing "an understanding remark to those who will be protesting." That suggestion was ignored, as were the protesters.

On April 30, Breger wrote a memo to Donald Regan in which he tried to explain "in capsule form, why the Bitburg wreath-laying stirs such emotions in the Jewish community."⁴⁹ Breger outlined two competing views of history that were integral in discussions surrounding the trip. He proposed that Chancellor Kohl and others "view the German people as having been controlled by a group of madmen during World War II." That view described the end of the war as a time of liberation for all Germans from the Nazis: "It is this version of history which the President will legitimate by the Bitburg wreath-laying." Breger proposed that there was a competing version of history that "holds that Germany was not led sullenly into the Nazi inferno by a few evil *madmen*. Rather, the entire nation was seized by a *totalitarian madness*" in which most Germans supported Hitler in the early stages of the war and were "willing participants in a patriotic war." That view of history would be rejected by a wreath laying. The acceptance of the second view dictated that "far more moral judgments must be made." Breger concluded by saying: "I believe that if the President has an appreciation of these competing views, he will be better able to engage in the reconciliation process for which he is making this trip."[50] Although Breger's arguments seemed strong, it is obvious in Reagan's speeches that he accepted the version of history that the Germans were controlled by a group of madmen led by one particularly mad person, Adolph Hitler. That decision virtually assured that the president's comments at Bergen-Belsen and Bitburg would not calm the frustration of Jewish opponents of the visit, because many of them rejected that view of history.

In the archives at the Reagan Library are two documents titled "President's Appearance at Bergen-Belsen."[51] One briefly lays out strategy for the visit: "The task is to organize the Bergen-Belsen ceremony in a fashion which makes the most of the President's strengths in communicating on a personal level. The goal should be to put together a dignified ceremony, with religious content, which concentrates on the human lessons of Bergen-Belsen for the past and the future." The document outlines four potential themes for the president's speech: the moral imperative symbolized by the Holocaust not only for Germans but for all humankind; the political imperative to ensure that conditions that made the Holocaust possible can never occur again; the lessons of peace that make it clear that the "fates of those less fortunate than ourselves" are not ignored; and the message of hope "carried by the process of healing which has taken place during the past forty years." The authors of this document call for a balance between the "lessons of the past and our vision for the future" and comment that the "ceremony should be solemn in character and not focus on current political issues." The president should praise "individual acts of selfishness and courage" that helped the healing process. A group of individuals should be invited who contributed to the healing process and some of them might be mentioned in the president's speech; a list of potential invitees is included. That suggestion was not accepted. No one on the list is mentioned in the speech, even though such acknowledgments were common in Reagan's speeches.

The second longer document seems to indicate a significant change in the focus of the trip. Under the section labeled "Strategy," it lists two tasks that should be achieved during the trip. The first proposes to make the Bergen-Belsen speech the "main event" on May 5: "By tailoring the organization, participation and content of the President's remarks to produce the highest profile media coverage, we should seek to consign the Bitburg visit to a secondary role." The second task is to develop a message that will "meet the concerns of groups" critical of the visit: "The public conclusion should be that through his sensitive and eloquent appearance at Bergen-Belsen, the President counterbalanced any negative results of a visit to the German war cemetery." The document suggests that one way to achieve this goal is to expand the understanding of the importance of the Bergen-Belsen visit beyond the Holocaust itself: "In addition to being one of the most important moral lessons of our time, the Holocaust symbolizes the unbroken tasks of free men everywhere." The speech should make it clear that conditions that led to the Holocaust could never occur again.

The authors of this memo argue that World War II was fought to allow democracy to flourish in Europe. The great success of the Federal Republic of Germany "demonstrates that we have been successful." Regrettably, though, there are still many places in Europe and the Soviet Union where "repression, intolerance, and mistreatment of minorities remain common." The Holocaust taught the world that peace cannot be assured under "conditions of repression." Therefore "we must maintain our sense of outrage at similar repression throughout the world today." Many of these themes did appear in the speeches on May 5. The issue of expressing outrage at repression in the world was particularly strong in the Bitburg speech.

This document places the president's remarks at the center of the Bergen-Belsen ceremony, but the Holocaust museum and memorials on the site could provide powerful visual images that would serve as an emotional backdrop for the speech. The president's remarks could be supported through the presence of invited individuals who "represent the themes the President wishes to stress." Again, a list of potential invitees was attached. The document also proposes the organization of a German-American dialogue on the Holocaust that would occur at the same time as the visit. The president and Chancellor Kohl could briefly participate in that discussion. The suggestion of having such a dialog was not accepted.

In the Reagan Library there are notes taken during a meeting held in the White House on April 25.[52] Several members of the staff including William Henkel and Marshall Breger were present. It is not clear who took the notes. The notes refer to the German trip as a "losing proposition" but propose that the administration "can turn it around." They make it clear that Reagan cannot be seen as honoring Nazis, so he has to redefine issues surrounding his visit. Three options for the redefinition are offered: show that Reagan never intended to honor Nazis and that the ceremony could be routine and include no one other than the United States; "tell strongest allie [sic], Mr. Kohl, that we think he is a leper and consequently, the visit is largely about us"; or "honor an allie [sic] [West Germany]." Obviously the third option was chosen, though it was unlikely that the other two were seriously considered. In conclusion the document states, "Don't curb short Bitburg visit time it's a confession of guilt." The notes clearly indicate that a great deal of discussion and deliberation were being given concerning the controversy and how to rescue the president's reputation from deteriorating even further.

Preparing the Speeches

In this heated atmosphere it was crucial that the speeches delivered at Bergen-Belsen and Bitburg be carefully written in an attempt to defuse the situation. Deaver describes the action taken to prepare these crucial speeches: "Once it became clear that the president was not open to suggestions that he cancel or cut back the trip, I knew that what he said there would in large measure determine how the passage to Bitburg would be judged. Ken Khachigian, a former Reagan speechwriter, was brought back" to write "the text of what the president would say. The theme was his [Reagan's] own. He wanted to put it in the context of where we had come in forty years."[53] Jose Gilder was selected to write the Bitburg speech.

The group meeting on April 25 began a discussion of potential themes for the speech and Reagan's physical movements and included potential visual images for television. Intriguingly, the notes reflect the controversy the president was facing because of his decision to visit the cemetery at Bitburg: "Try to redeem this day from the ashes." This ashes theme later became a significant one in the Bergen-Belsen speech when Reagan uttered: "Out of ashes, hope." The notes also contain what might be seen as the central theme of the day: "From Bergen Belsen to Bitburg—From the past to the present." Those words appear in the Bitburg speech and could be seen as a thesis of the speech.[54]

The April 25 notes refer to both speeches: "Identify tangible examples—people there—quiet heroes" and "The speech fit w/(with) themes of other speeches. Especially Strasburg [speech to European Parliament during the visit]." The interest in quiet heroes was reflected in many Reagan speeches. The speeches at the ceremonies at Normandy the previous year were classic examples of how he recognized such people. The files at the Reagan Library indicate the lengths the staff went to study the locations for the speeches in West Germany and the people who would be present. There was a careful effort to find individuals who might be honored in the speeches, but in the end no one was mentioned except at Bitburg and then only briefly.

The notes from April 25 seem to indicate that most of the time and energy in the meeting focused on Bergen-Belsen, again an indication of the shifting emphasis of the trip from Bitburg to Bergen-Belsen. The notes propose that the speech be brief, only three to ten minutes long. A passage in the document reflects a theme that appears in the Bergen-Belsen speech: "Leadership of German Govt. (Government) will be there—the political elite of modern-day Germany." There is a discussion of potential visual aspects of the event. The group planned to have the President and Mrs. Reagan "walk over ½ mile through camp," the camp is "wooded" with "tall pines." The walk would take them "through forest & come into an opening" with "heather all around."

Heather is mentioned once again: "Heather—symbolism?" But then a note of caution is added: "may not be in bloom." The notes briefly describes the mounds where people are buried, the main Jewish memorial, an "oblisk" with "inscriptions 7 or 8 languages" surrounded by "100 private family memorials, scattered about." Reagan should walk around the mounds, then the memorial, and deliver "very brief non-denominational comments."

One of the participants in the meeting, Marshall Breger, again recommends that the Kaddish, the "memorial prayer for the dead," be said at the beginning of the program. This is a theme Berger reiterated on many occasions as a way to lessen Jewish criticism of the event. The leaders should then place wreaths, Kohl would speak, then Reagan, and then they would "walk to a landing zone & depart."

The notes conclude with other important ideas and potential themes:

Research: examples of personalities that can be mentioned & people in the audience
Rehabilitation & healing—
Ann Frank—forgiveness—[Is] Her father still alive [?]
You can destroy forever in all people for all time a spark of humanity.
Be careful about humanizing [the Nazis, particularly Hitler].

The ideas for the speech at Bitburg are much briefer. They contain a mention that Bitburg is in the area of "Kohl's political base." The speech should last seven or eight minutes. There are also words that seem to indicate the prevailing conditions at Bitburg: "somber, cloudy, stark, wind blows." The description states that Reagan and Kohl will go from the "cordon outside," walk into "cemetery & lay wreath" proceed "to motorcade back to Base where they will view United States and German troops," and then to a hangar at the military base where they will do lunch with troops and "some people from the community." The section concludes that there is a "State dinner at Bonn that night."

On the next day, April 26, speechwriter Ken Khachigian, Michael

Deaver, and William Henkel, Deaver's successor and "an experienced advance man,"[55] met with Reagan to begin the process of writing the Bergen-Belsen speech. Khachigian was struck by Reagan's appearance: "He remembered from the Nixon days what a wounded President looked like, and found himself looking at another."[56] This meeting illustrates the importance of the speech inasmuch as Reagan did not always meet face to face with speechwriters and usually did not take on such a prominent role.

Morris described the meeting: "For twenty-five minutes, Khachigian sat scribbling in amazement. Normally, Reagan needed to be coaxed into the mood of a speech by staff tossing phrases at him; today, he was impatient of interruption. Only when the Oval Office clock struck five did the interview end." Reagan stressed the ideas he wanted included in the speech. Khachigian believed that he already had an opening with the theme of "No one of us can understand" and a conclusion, "Never again." In order to get more ideas for the speech, he "asked White House researchers to comb through travel guides and the Talmud, but his imagination remained locked until an advance man returning from Bergen-Belsen mentioned that the local countryside . . . was 'greening' with spring. Words, or the feel of words, began to come." The speech crystallized even more a few days later "when Khachigian attended a service at Arlington National Cemetery for his Armenian forebears, massacred by the Turks seventy years before. A sudden sense of ethnic suffering possessed him, and he hurried back to the hotel to write."[57]

Many of the themes of the speech emerged from the meeting with Reagan, but there are interesting ideas in the notes that are not used in the speech. One lengthy passage makes the point that "after a war, always left with the seeds of the next war. . . . It's the fact that after WW I peace treaty punished Germany and we planted the seeds for a later war. This time 7 nations summit—3 of them were former enemies. No stronger allies than [Yasuhiro] Nakasone (of Japan) and Kohl (with the exception of Maggie Thatcher)." Although this theme did not appear in the Bergen-Belsen speech, it was included in the Bitburg speech.[58]

The notes also include a discussion of how to describe the actions of the German people after World War II: "They don't try to erase the memory. They try to erase the shame." Written next to these sentences is the statement, "'erase' maybe not the right word." In the delivered text, "erase" does not appear but the phrase "confront and condemn" does. Deaver recommended that the group "see if places of worship which were destroyed are restored. Talk about it." Henkel proposed that the speech "pat the German people on the back for stepping up to it." Reagan added this lengthy passage: "I find myself thinking . . . But we killed those people. Are we holding a grudge. Should we say: all of these people have met the supreme judge & they will be judged by Him who has the only right to do that." He added, "Remember that there were Germans who resisted & lost their lives." An additional point was, "[people from] 23 countries—[are] buried at Bergen-Belsen."

There is an undated document in the Reagan Library that contains further notes for the speech and begins to illustrate the extensive use of antithesis and balance that eventually was used in the final speech.[59] The author, probably Khachigian, was trying out phrases that might appear in the speech: "From Horror to Hope"; "from devastation to . . ."; "from . . . to possibility." The author returns to the phrase that in some respects could be seen as the main theme of the speech: "Out of ashes—hope." There are also two sections that do not appear in any of the drafts of the speech: "Music and art in camps—Lyric beauty of the art that gave expression to hope even as their prison physically appeared to belie that hope," and "Some say that this means that man is inevitably corrupt—that we are consigned forever to a world where these horrors can occur again. If that is true, then why are we here?" The document introduces the theme of the death of children at the camps, a theme that grew in importance with each version of the speech and became a central part of the final text. The document also introduces the theme of spring with its rebirth and renewal—again, a theme that became more important and central in the final draft.

There are two other intriguing documents in this folder that relate to the writing of the speech. A plastic envelope contains a napkin from "Clyde's An American Bar" with writing on it and a cover note from Ken K(hachigian) to Nancy Reagan dated 9–3-85 in which the writer states: "The napkin—believe it or not—is where I came up with the idea for the end of the speech, while waiting to have dinner one night." The notes on the napkin include: "(1). Somewhere here—at Bergen-Belsen lies Anne Frank. Everywhere here is a memory—pulling at us; touching us—making us—realize that such memories never wear down—never flag. They take us where God intended man to go—towards (2) learning—towards healing—towards redemption." The note continues, "show the endless sketch of our heart—Unfailing capacity for change & knowing commitment that each one of us can make the world better." There is also stationery from "The Madison" in Washington, D.C., that includes a draft of the ideas in the last paragraph of the speech. The paper has the word "witness" followed by "man doesn't prevail—it's the core of hope that rests in each human soul. It's what our President Lincoln called "'the better angels of our nature.'"

A second plastic envelope contains a large manila envelope that proposes words that did not appear in the speech but contain powerful images of the brutality of Hitler's soldiers: "They came in the night—men in boots & brown shirts & they dragged them from their homes—the sleeping tailor, the old man of 72 & young man of 17 & they...." It also contains four other points: the State of Israel came out of the suffering of World War II, "one good thing"; the name of the Israeli ambassador to Germany; the "Plight of Jewry worldwide—those who can't leave" their countries, especially in the Soviet Union; and the fact that 50,000 Soviet soldiers "who were dispatched to German died at Bergen-Belsen."

The envelope also contains wording that has the potential to become the opening of the speech: "(1) No one of the rest of us can completely understand the feelings of victims of the camps & the prisons—they will have memory beyond a/tg (anything) we can recognize or imagine. Recognize this. (2) But imp. (imply) that we remember the holocaust for the purpose of insuring that it never happens again." "Everybody on all sides—whether under crosses or stars of david—whole world were victims of this evil that started w/ (with) Hitler."

Khachigian had a complete draft of the speech on April 28. The draft contains most of the themes and much of the language of the final speech. One major section includes a passage from "the Mourner's

Kaddish—the Jewish Memorial Prayer to the dead": "Be not afraid of sudden terror, nor of the storm that strikes the wicked. Form your plot—it shall fail; lay your plan—it shall not prevail. For God is with us." Although Marshall Breger lobbied hard for its inclusion, the prayer did not appear in the final speech. It was deleted from the text in a revision on April 29.[60]

This first draft and the subsequent revisions illustrate the steps Khachigian took in writing the speech. Each draft of the speech has a significant number of proposed revisions, additions, and deletions in Khachigian's handwriting. For example, early in the speech Khachigian had written, "Their anguish and agony were pressed on them only because of the object of their prayers and the accident of their birth." In the next draft, he changed two words in the sentence: "Their anguish and agony were pressed on them only because of the **God in** their prayers and the accident of their birth." The final speech kept the edit and significantly altered the wording: "Their **pain was borne only because of who they were and** because of the God in their prayers." Later in the speech, Khachigian wrote: "And too many of them knew that this was their fate. Their faith kept them strong—but in some, there was a conspicuous spirit that moved their faith." The language was changed to "And too many of them knew that this was their fate. **Rising out of this was a strong faith and** a conspicuous spirit that moved their faith." In this case, the final draft did not include this edit: "And too many of them knew that this was their fate, but that was not the end. Through it all was their faith and a spirit that moved their faith."[61]

Khachigian again made significant changes in a draft that is dated April 29, 1985. A copy of that draft contains significant editing in Khachigian's handwriting.[62] For example, the opening paragraph of the speech contains the following words: "This painful walk back into time has done much more than remind us of the war that consumed the European continent more than four decades ago." The editing alters the paragraph: "This painful walk into **the past** has done much more than remind us of the war that consumed the European continent." This language appears in the final text. The draft also contains an interesting passage in which Khachigian edited his own words. The first draft of the speech contains the following passage. "I think we must probably all think of the same thing first. What about the youngsters brought into the boundaries of this stalag." The first revision changes the passage significantly: "**All of us** probably **share** the same first **thoughts**. What **about** the youngsters brought into the boundaries of this **dark** stalag? In the April 29 version he changes it again: "**I'm sure we all** share similar first thoughts. **And that is:** What of the youngsters brought within the boundaries of this dark stalag?" Much of the language is incorporated into the final speech: "I'm sure we all share similar first thoughts, and that is: What of the youngsters who died at this dark stalag?" This passage is significant because it is the only time in the speech that the speechwriter has Reagan speak in first person.

Khachigian again made changes in a draft labeled "April 29, 1985, 10:00 A.M." He edited the speech by changing a few words and deleting some sections. The most significant change was to move the section about young people mentioned above to a place much earlier in the speech, where it remained. This change significantly strengthened the focus of the speech on young people who died in the camps and set up the later discussion of Anne Frank and her ideas. This draft was also carefully examined for style, accuracy of quotes, and accuracy of information.

Later on that same day, Khachigian produced another copy that included his revisions.[63] The draft was labeled "Master" and was circulated to Regan, Deaver, Patrick Buchanan, and Robert McFarlane. At the bottom is a note: "Please provide *your personal* edits directly to Ken Khachigian . . . by 10:00 a.m tomorrow, with an information copy to my office. We plan to forward a draft to the President at noon tomorrow, 4/30." The master copy reflects some minor revisions that must have been suggested by the readers. The most significant change is in a passage that was significantly revised in earlier drafts: "Here lie people—**Jews**—whose death was inflicted for no **reason** other than their very existence. Their pain was borne only because of who they were and because of the God in their prayers. **Alongside them lie many Christians**." The final draft underwent minor changes: "Here lie people—Jews—whose death was inflicted for no reason other than their very existence. Their pain was borne only because of who they were and because of the God in their prayers. Alongside them **lay** many Christians—**Catholics and Protestants.**"

The next draft is dated April 30, 1985, at 2:00 P.M. It contains several minor changes in wording. At this point, specific references to Hitler by name are eliminated and he is referred to as "that man" or "one man." Perhaps the biggest change is the tone of the language. Here is an example: "Above all, we are struck by the waste of it all—the horrible, inglorious, incomprehensible waste." Notice how the language becomes more vivid: "Above all, we are struck by the **horror** of it all—the **monstrous**, incomprehensible **horror**." That same language is present in the final draft.

The papers at the Reagan Library contain a virtually final draft that is dated 9:00 A.M. (FRG) May 4, 1985.[64] There were some minor changes in spelling but at this point the speech was ready for the president's delivery.

There are not as many drafts of the Bitburg speech in the archives as there are of the Bergen-Belsen speech. Reagan did not meet with Josh Gilder before he wrote the speech, so there are no notes as there were for the Bergen-Belsen speech. The examples that are available provide some interesting insights into Gilder's thought processes.

Gilder joined the speechwriting staff on April 1, so he was new to the position when he was assigned the speech.[65] He was given the task because the speech was originally seen as not being important, "just a drop by" that would not even receive much press attention. Once the controversy escalated, however, the situation in the White House became impossible. Gilder expected that the speech would be given to a more experienced person because of its increased importance. He felt tremendous tension in the White House. Many people, including Gilder, thought that Reagan was wrong in his decision to visit the cemetery and that he was being too stubborn in either not changing his agenda or canceling the trip to Bitburg. Gilder said that many of his colleagues avoided him because they felt sorry for him having to write such an important speech and knew that he was under great pressure to produce an effective document.

Gilder listened to everything Reagan said during the controversy and talked to everyone he could, including Marshall Breger, in order to prepare the speech. As he listened to Reagan's speeches and press conferences, Gilder began to believe that he was right in his decision to take the journey to Bitburg. Gilder also came to believe that the speech at Bergen-Belsen was not nearly as important as the one at Bitburg in spite of the fact that many other members of the staff seemed to be focusing their time and energy on Bergen-Belsen. It became clear to him that Reagan was telling the public that they could not continue to hold all Germans guilty for the events of World War II, that it was not the American way to continue to blame everyone. Reagan was afraid that he might radicalize and demoralize younger generations of Germans by blaming them for something that happened before they were born. Reagan believed that Kohl was a bulwark against communist attempts to split NATO and the European allies; he had to support Kohl in a manner that would make it clear that he could trust Reagan. The speech at Bitburg was an opportunity to give such strong assurances.

In Gilder's view, Reagan saw the Nazis as one form of evil but the Soviets as another. Reagan was calling upon the world to move the focus from the Nazis to the Soviets and other contemporary tyrants, from the Gestapo to the cold war. The speech was being delivered at a military base so that Reagan would be honoring the U.S. military and the German military. Reagan saw the past forty years as a great story, a story of how a country moved from being fascist to democratic; he saw that other countries could follow that path.

Gilder described writing drafts and then showing them to the other speechwriters and members of the White House staff. He did not see Reagan until the manuscript was complete, but Reagan was pleased with the speech.

There are two copies of the speech labeled "Master" and dated April 29, 1985, 6:00 P.M.[66] One has suggested editing, the other has the same comments as the first but with additional suggested revisions from a second person, most of which were not accepted. It is not clear who suggested the comments or why they were ignored. By April 29, most of the speech was finalized, but there were two significant additions, both in the form of a story. There was also some reorganization of the paragraphs.

The first insertion occurs early in the speech when Reagan is reaching out to the veterans of World War II and their families. In the speech draft, Gilder has Reagan conclude his comments to the veterans by saying that the democratic nations of Europe stand "as living testimony that their noble sacrifice was not in vain." The speech then moves to addressing the survivors of the Holocaust. In the final speech delivered at Bitburg, there is an addition that repeats the refrain, "No, their sacrifice was not in vain." Gilder has Reagan describe in first person how he was filled with hope when U.S. general Matthew B. Ridgway and German general Johannes Steinhoff met in the German cemetery and "reconciled and united for freedom. They reached over the graves to one another like brothers and grasped their hands in peace." This story would make the reconciliation between the United States and Germany concrete in a simple gesture of two former enemies in World War II. It would also add a significant amount of emotion to the speech.

The speech then reaches out to the survivors of the Holocaust by saying that the reconciliation with West Germany does not mean that the Holocaust has been forgotten. Where Reagan speaks to the survivors, there is one sentence that goes through a minor change, but the wording makes the meaning more significant. In the draft the sentence reads: "I have just come this morning from Bergen-Belsen, where the horror of that momentous crime was forever burned upon my memory." In the speech that was delivered in Bitburg, the text is slightly altered: "I have just come this morning from Bergen-Belsen, where the horror of that **terrible** crime, **the Holocaust,** was forever burned upon my memory." The wording makes the actions of the Nazis even worse and reiterates that the horrible crime was the Holocaust.

The draft speech refers to Hitler by name, but his name does not appear in the speech as delivered. The first mention of Hitler states, "The war against Hitler was not like other wars." At Bitburg, Reagan says, "The war against **one man's totalitarian dictatorship** was not like other wars." Later the draft asks, "How many were followers of Hitler who willfully carried out his cruel orders?" The final speech changes the question somewhat: "How many were **fanatical** followers of **a dictator and** willfully carried out his cruel orders?" As at Bergen-Belsen, Reagan refuses to use Hitler's name but describes him in terms that make him and his actions seem even more evil.

The most significant change in the speech is the insertion of a lengthy story about an emotional World War II event. Gilder did not remember who gave him the idea for the story, but it is a moving one and one that Reagan could use as a secular preacher to teach a lesson to the audience.[67] In the speech Reagan speaks of how out of the ruins of war has grown an atmosphere of peace between the United States and Germany. Bitburg Air Base is a symbol of that peace and a symbol of a better future between the two nations. He then moves to tell the story: "The hope we see now could sometimes even be glimpsed in the darkest day of the war. I'm thinking of one special story—that of a mother and her young son living alone in a modest cottage in the middle of the woods."

There are two drafts of the text of the story in the Reagan Library, labeled "Gilder/Khachigian Edits, April 30, 1985, 11:30 A.M.[68] The story concerns the chance meeting of U.S. and German soldiers during the Battle of the Bulge in a small cabin in the wood in which a mother and her small son lived. The mother tells the soldiers there will be no violence on that night and feeds them some of her last food. The next day the soldiers return to their own lines and the war continues as before. The meeting was on Christmas Eve 1944.

I discuss this story at length in chapter 4, but it is intriguing to see the changes made in the editing. One significant sentence went through several revisions. In one draft the sentence first reads, "Now, listen to the story through the eyes of the woman's young son." The sentence is changed to "Now, listen to the story through the eyes of one who was there." Gilder keeps the sentence in his draft but it is dramatically revised in the final speech: "**But** now, listen to the **rest of** the story through the eyes of one who was there, **now a grown man, but that young lad that had been her son.**"

The most significant change in the story is the introduction. In the first draft, the story opens in a matter-of-fact way: "A story about a German woman and her boy, alone in a farm house as the Battle of the Bulge raged around them. They heard a knock on the door and there in the snow stood three young American soldiers—lost behind enemy lines." The second draft is more descriptive and interesting: "Even during the darkest days of the War, there was sometimes hope. There's a story of a German boy and his mother who lived alone in a farm house—it couldn't have been too far from here. One night, the Battle of the Bulge raging around them, they heard a knock on the door." Gilder rejected that draft and wrote a new one. The final draft first appeared in handwritten form and then was inserted into the text: "The hope we see now could sometimes even be glimpsed in the darkest days of the war. I'm thinking of one special story—that of a mother and her young son living alone in a modest cottage in the middle of the woods. And one night as the Battle of the Bulge exploded not far away, and around them, three young American soldiers arrived at their door—they were standing there in the snow, lost behind enemy lines." This final draft is even more descriptive and Reagan the storyteller steps forward and tells the story in the first person.

There is also a notable change in the paragraph that follows the story. Reagan speaks directly to the men and women at Bitburg Air Base and to the German residents of Bitburg. In the draft he addresses the Americans first and then the Germans. In the final speech he reverses the order and speaks to the Germans first and then the Americans. This would seem a fitting order—to first acknowledge your hosts and then your own soldiers.

The text now comes to what Gilder sees as the most important section of the message, the part in which Reagan talks about the importance of moving from the focus on Nazis to contemporary tyrants. An earlier draft has the following line: "Four decades ago, we waged a great war to push back the shadow of evil from the world, to let men and women in this country live in the light of liberty." The sentence is revised to place more emphasis on the light/dark imagery that forms such an important part of the speech: "Four decades ago, we waged a great war to **lift** the **darkness** of evil from the world, to let men and women in this country and in every county live in the **sunshine** of liberty." The next sentence notes that Germany, Italy, and Japan are now free nations, but Reagan cautions that freedom in not complete because many people in the world still live in totalitarianism.

Gilder believes that the next paragraph forms the crux of the message, expressing the need for everyone in the world to see themselves as potential victims of totalitarianism. The paragraph begins with a reference to the famous speech by John F. Kennedy in 1963 near the Berlin Wall in which Kennedy proclaimed that he too was a Berliner. Reagan extends that theme to the present. The sentence goes through minor revisions from the draft to the delivered version. The sections that were eliminated are highlighted here: "Today **all** freedom-loving people around the world must say, I am a Berliner, I am a Jew in a world still threatened by anti-semitism, I am an Afghanistani, and I am a prisoner of the Gulag, I am a refugee in [a] **an over**-crowded boat floundering off the coast of Vietnam, I am a Laotian, a Cambodian, a Cuban, and a Miskito Indian; I too, am a potential victim of totalitarianism." Next to the paragraph is written the word "good."

Reagan continues to say that the one lesson that should have been learned from World War II is that freedom must be stronger than totalitarianism. He states that Germany is an example of that freedom and extends the idea by saying that lessons learned from the past can be used to make a better future. The future is obviously one in which democracy defeats totalitarianism.

In the conclusion to the speech there is one final major change. Reagan concludes his presentation by talking about how the events of this historic anniversary give the world hope. The draft describes the freedom that is sweeping the globe in Latin America, Asia, and the Middle East, and in Europe and America the hope is growing stronger. In the speech as delivered, Reagan talks about hope and a sentence is inserted into the text that illustrates that hope. The sentence is strangely awkward, as though Reagan made an error and then corrected himself: "One of the symbols of that hate—that could have been that hope, a little while ago, when we heard a German band playing the American National Anthem and an American band playing the German National Anthem." This sentence simply is not as clear and carefully structured as the rest of the speech.

Like the Bergen-Belsen speech, the one in Bitburg was carefully checked for potential errors in language and facts. A final draft was written and ready for delivery. Now Reagan had to deliver the speeches effectively in Germany.

Preparing for the Journey

On the evening of his departure, Reagan outlined the goals of his trip to members of his staff by stating that he would be attending the economic summit in Bonn and making state visits in Germany, Spain, and Portugal.[69] He was also scheduled to speak to the European Parliament in Strasbourg, France, "to mark the 40th anniversary of the end of the Second World War in Europe and the beginning of an unprecedented period of peace and prosperity." In his comments he said, "Forty years ago, World War II was nearing its end, much of Europe lay in ruins. The destruction and terrible human losses were matched by fear and doubt about an uncertain future." He contrasted that Europe with one "that is rebuilt from the disaster of war and morally restored from the despair of 1945. The strong, confident alliance of free people who've done this can take satisfaction in those achievements and look forward to the future with confidence. So, we leave on this journey infused with pride and hope."

On May 4, 1985, Reagan spoke to the nation about the Bonn economic summit.[70] His words reflect his many previous comments: "This year's summit is winding up on the eve of the 40th anniversary of the end of World War II. As is fitting, we celebrate the remarkable achievements of the world's family of free nations during these last four decades: peace has flourished; our economies have prospered, and technological advances have revolutionized our lives." He continues: "The friendly atmosphere of our meeting made it difficult to imagine that the United States, France, Britain, and Canada were pitted against countries which today are among freedom's staunchest supporters—the Federal Republic of Germany, Japan, and Italy. We celebrate our shared success, and we take heart that former enemies have been reconciled and are now partners and friends."

The stage was now set for the dramatic events of May 5, 1985.

CHAPTER 4

From the Ashes Has Come Hope

May 5, 1985, was a difficult but important day in Ronald Reagan's presidency. On that day, Reagan attempted to answer the many critics who questioned his motives in visiting a concentration camp and a German military cemetery. Reagan hoped that two well-prepared and well-delivered speeches would calm many of his critics while inspiring his supporters.

The Reagans began their day with an unscheduled journey to lay flowers on the grave of Konrad Adenauer, West Germany's first chancellor. Officials said that the idea had come from evangelist Billy Graham.[1] The visit to Adenauer's grave was part of the effort to silence Reagan's critics. The trip would be a symbolic one that would remind Germans of this revered figure and his efforts in leading the country during its transition from the Nazi reign to democracy. The visit would also serve as a sign of reconciliation between the United States and Germany as well as a message to Reagan's critics that he was not just honoring German war dead but also remembering the generation that created democracy in West Germany and those who had successfully challenged the Nazis. In the planning leading up to the speeches on May 5, there had been discussions of including references to Adenauer, but the writers chose not to mention him. After the stop at Adenauer's grave, the Reagans and Kohls flew to Hanover and then rode in a helicopter to Bergen-Belsen.

The Speech at Bergen-Belsen

The visit to Bergen-Belsen forced Reagan to confront the kind of emotional situation he had not handled well in the past. As Lou Cannon said, Reagan "could deal with scenes of death related to a heroic purpose, as at Normandy, but he was helpless in the presence of genocide."[2] Nancy Reagan and Michael Deaver knew that Reagan was not able to function well in depressing circumstances. They kept remembering an event during the 1980 campaign: "At a veterans home in Indiana early in the 1980 campaign, Reagan had been overcome at the sight of the ailing and aged veterans who had been assembled to hear him and had literally been unable to complete his speech. Nancy Reagan, seeing him falter, stepped forward and smoothly completed the speech for him, only later expressing her fury at the local politician who had brought them there."[3] With incidents like that vivid in her mind, Nancy Reagan strongly opposed visiting a concentration camp, as she had during his previous European trips. She was overruled because the political atmosphere surrounding Reagan's visit to Bitburg made it imperative that he agree to a stop at a concentration camp like Bergen-Belsen.

Reagan entered the camp "under gray skies and in a light drizzle," as described by Edmund Morris.[4] There were demonstrators outside the camp, some of whom asked Reagan not to enter the site. He ignored their request. Inside, the premier of Lower Saxony, Ernst Albrecht, "escorted the Kohls and their entourage into a document center with photographs and exhibits of the camp, where Jewish, Gypsy, Polish, Russian, French and Dutch inmates died of torture, starvation and disease. As the Reagans paused in front of a photograph of stacks of bodies discovered by the British, who liberated the camp in April 1945, Reagan put his arm around his wife." According to Morris, the Reagans forced "themselves to look at blowups of white, stork-limbed, tangled corpses." Another observed noted that "members of Mr. Reagan's staff looked grim during the visit. Robert C. McFarlane, the national security advisor, walked alone, staring at the ground."⁵ Cannon described Reagan as "a shaken man as he toured the camp and saw the photographs of the stacks of bodies of the human beings who had died at Bergen-Belsen. A reporter noticed that he kept his arm around Nancy Reagan, 'partly to steer her and partly, it appeared, to derive some support from her presence.' Somehow, Reagan made it through the tour and delivered his speech."⁶

Chancellor Kohl spoke before Reagan. His brief speech was somber and somewhat awkward, as though he seemed uncomfortable in the setting. At the beginning of the speech Kohl presented a historical view of World War II similar to the one Reagan would offer in his comments: "You have come here to pay homage to the victims of National Socialist tyranny. Bergen-Belsen was a place of unimaginable atrocities. It was only one of the many sites testifying to a demonic will to destroy."⁷ It was obvious that the two leaders agreed on a common interpretation of World War II, that the war was caused by a group of corrupt Nazi leaders who convinced the majority of Germans to follow them.

Kohl noted that he as chancellor had "professed our historical responsibility" for the events that occurred at Bergen-Belsen in a German ceremony two weeks earlier. He honored U.S. soldiers who helped liberate Europe and "lost their lives in that act of liberation." He then described Germans bowing "in sorrow before the victims of murder and genocide." He concluded: "The supreme goal of our political efforts is to render impossible any repetition of that systematic destruction of human life and dignity. With their partners and friends, the Americans and Germans therefore stand together as allies in the community of shared values and in the defense alliance in order to safeguard man's absolute and inviolable dignity in conditions of freedom and peace."

Reagan's speech was carefully researched, organized, and written. Reagan knew that he faced tremendous pressure in placating his many critics in the United States, especially in the Jewish community and among veterans of World War II and their families. Realistically, he could not overcome all the frustration and anger felt by his detractors, but he might somewhat calm them if his message contained the right words and was delivered in the proper tone. The speech was not a lengthy one, but Reagan faced a difficult task in the few minutes he spoke.[8]

Reagan begins with a standard recognition of his hosts, "Chancellor Kohl and honored guests," and then moves into a description of the deep and painful emotions of the day: "This painful walk into the past has done much more than remind us of the war that consumed the European Continent. What we have seen makes it unforgettably clear that no one of the rest of us can fully understand the enormity of the feelings carried by the victims of these camps." The language in this sentence seems a bit unusual and awkward. The speechwriter chose "no one of the rest of us" rather than "none of us" intentionally; the phrase appears in all the drafts of the speech. But it seems awkward and overly wordy for such a brief speech.

Reagan speaks directly to the survivors of the concentration camps in an attempt to reach out to them and show them and their supporters that he really cares about them, in spite of critics charging that he has forgotten the suffering the survivors had endured: "The survivors carry a memory beyond anything that we can comprehend. The awful evil started by one man, an evil that victimized all the world with its destruction, was uniquely destructive of the millions forced into the grim abyss of these camps." In earlier drafts of the speech Hitler had been mentioned by name, but Reagan does not use Hitler's name at Bergen-Belsen. Hitler's form of evil was so extraordinary that the mere mention of his name would desecrate the setting; Reagan would not acknowledge him as a person worthy of mention. The wording makes Hitler a less important person and does not "humanize" him, as suggested in the documents planning the speech. Similar language appears later in the text when Reagan talks about "that man and his evil." References claiming that one man had caused the enormous destruction and suffering in World War II show that Reagan accepted the historical interpretation of the war as caused by Hitler and his fanatical followers, not by the majority of Germans. This view could be interpreted to mean that most Germans were innocent or victims of corrupt leaders. Critics could be upset by this choice of language since it freed most Germans from the guilt caused by the events of World War II, including many of the soldiers buried at Bitburg.

The structure of the sentences throughout much of the speech is carefully organized so that words are repeated in successive clauses, giving them even more emphasis and power. For example, in the first clause of one of the sentences mentioned above, the words "awful evil" are used—not just evil but "awful evil," followed in the second clause with "an evil." The second half of the sentence repeats the word "destruction," followed by "uniquely destructive" of millions who were forced into "the grim abyss." The words "uniquely destructive" would imply that the events that occurred in the camps were unlike anything in the history of the world, therefore making Hitler's crimes even more unimaginable. Throughout the speech the writer carefully chose adjectives like "awful" and "grim" in an attempt to make the actions of Hitler and the other Nazis seem worse than other war criminals in history.

Reagan moves to the reason inmates were forced into this horrible circumstance: "Here lie people—Jews—whose death was inflicted for no reason other than their very existence. Their pain was borne only because of who they were and because of the God in their prayers." He acknowledges, however, that not only Jews died in the camps: "Alongside them lay many Christians—Catholics and Protestants." It is notable that he specifically makes references to both Catholics and Protestants, as though he were educating his audience as to who could be included as Christians. These prisoners in the camps, no matter their religious affiliation, died because of the actions of one man and his followers. In a vivid passage Reagan describes the horrendous events that occurred while Hitler was in power: "Hell yawned forth its awful contents." The word "awful" is intriguing. It appears earlier in the speech in an "awful evil." It is difficult to imagine anything worse than evil, but "awful evil" or "awful contents" go beyond the normal comprehension of people, again making Hitler's actions even worse. In parallel language he describes what happened to those individuals who were prisoners in the camp: "People were brought here for no other purpose but to suffer and die—to go unfed when hungry, uncared for when sick, tortured when the whim struck, and left to have misery consume them when all there was around them was misery." Parallel structure is used throughout the speech to create a kind of beauty and rhythm to the language. The language of each clause builds on the previous one, leading to a climax at the end of the sentence.

Reagan makes that misery seem even worse by focusing on the young people who died in the camps. By highlighting the torture and deaths of the young, he makes the actions of the Nazis seem even more criminal. This focus on youth foreshadows the powerful story of Anne Frank in the second half of the speech. Reagan switches to first person and asks a question: "I'm sure we all share similar first thoughts, and that is: 'What of the youngsters who died at this dark stalag?'" The use of "stalag," typically defined as a German prison camp for noncommissioned or enlisted prisoners of war, makes the setting seem even more ominous. He contrasts the evil and the dark with vivid images of warmth, light, and pain: "All was gone for them forever—not to feel again the warmth of life's sunshine and promise, not the laughter and splendid ache of growing up, nor the consoling embrace of a family. Try to think of being young and never having a day without searing emotional and physical pain—desolate, unrelieved pain." Again, the repetition of the word "pain" builds the power of the image in the audience's mind. Words like "pain," "feeling," and "ache" are repeated throughout the text. Reagan uses an intriguing adjective in the phrase "splendid ache." The listener not only hears about the suffering of those who were forced into the camps but can also share the suffering through other senses, particularly the sense of touch.

He moves away from the suffering of young people briefly but returns to it at the end of the speech. He reiterates the horror of the camps, particularly the horror created by the commandant of the camp—"the Beast of Belsen." Again the person's name, Josef Kramer, is not mentioned because it would desecrate the day and Kramer is less of a person when his name is not used. To heighten the feeling of horror, Reagan again uses repetition of words—first a sentence with repetition of the word "horror" followed by a longer phrase using the words "feel" and "felt." "Above all, we're struck by the horror of it—the monstrous, incomprehensible horror. And that's what we've seen but is what we can never understand as the victims did." The words "feel" and "felt" are repeated to allow the audience to try to experience many of the same emotions, but those present can not understand the suffering of the victims: "Nor with all our compassion can we feel what the survivors feel to this day and what they will feel for as long as they live. What we've felt and are expressing with words cannot convey the suffering they endured." The repetition of the word "feel" is an attempt to go beyond simply hearing and to extend the suffering to other senses. This language, again, attempts to tell survivors that Reagan is concerned with their plight and will never forget them.

Reagan punctuates his text with the shocking words "Here death ruled." But he is not content to stop with this harsh statement. He will not dwell only on the negative. His natural spirit of optimism does not allow Reagan to let the situation remain so negative and hopeless. He proposes that people can overcome even the harshest of settings: "We found that death cannot rule forever, and that's why we're here today." There is a lesson to be learned from the deaths of the inmates, and he describes that lesson in a series of parallel statements: "We're here because humanity refused to accept that freedom of the spirit of man can ever be extinguished. We're here to commemorate that life triumphed over the tragedy and the death of the Holocaust—overcame the suffering, the sickness, the testing, and, yes, the gassings. We're here today to confirm that the horror cannot outlast hope and even from the worst of all things, the best may come forth." His optimism is constantly repeated through the use of hope—even in the most dire of situations there is always hope in Reagan's mind and in his rhetoric. That hope comes through in the lesson Reagan offers, which is based on his spiritual beliefs. Reagan assumes the role of secular preacher talking to all people in the world: "Even out of this overwhelming sadness, there must be some purpose and there is. It comes to us through the transforming love of God."

As secular preacher he turns to the sacred Jewish text, the Talmud, for support of his ideas of hope and renewal: "It was only through suffering that the children of Israel obtained three priceless and coveted gifts: The

Torah, the land of Israel, and the World to come." He continues: "Yes, out of this sickness—as crushing and cruel as it was—there was hope for the world as well as the world to come. Out of the ashes—hope, and from all the pain—promise." If there is one sentence in the speech that expresses his overall theme, this is the sentence. In some respects this sentence also describes his purpose for giving the speech: to lift the image of his administration out of the ashes and move forward toward a better world full of hope once this conflict over his current visit is forgotten.

This sentence may be seen as a vehicle to move to a more positive picture, and it presents a kind of transition in the tone of the presentation. The first half of the speech focuses on the horrors and suffering of the past. Although there is still some discussion of evil in the second half, Reagan seems to be building toward a better future and a better life in that future for all people in the world.

He says that the promise of a better world is illustrated by the fact that the political leadership of West Germany is present at the occasion. Those leaders are a contrast to the evil individuals who ruled Germany during World War II. He congratulates Chancellor Kohl and the other leaders for making "real the renewal that had to happen." He praises them for their courage in confronting and condemning the "acts of a hated regime of the past." Again he avoids the use of specific names, as though their mention would pollute the occasion and the memory of those who died at this spot. The actions of the present German leaders reflect "the courage of your people and their devotion to freedom and justice since the war." He asks the audience to "think how far we've come from that time when despair made these tragic victims wonder if anything could survive." His picture of the progress since World War II is a positive one, but he looks forward to one of even more growth and progress.

He moves to a theme of rebirth and renewal. The world did survive the horrors of the past, as can be seen in the contrast between the bleakness and ugliness of the lives of those in the camp and the beauty of spring and the rebirth of life in Germany of 1985: "As we flew here from Hanover, low over the greening farms and the emerging springtime of the lovely German countryside, I reflected, and there must have been a time when the prisoners at Bergen-Belsen and those of every other camp must have felt that the springtime was gone forever." But the prisoners did not have Reagan's hindsight to see that life would continue and there would be rebirth. They could not have his hope or see the promise of a new life: "Surely we can understand that what we see around us—all these children of God under bleak and lifeless mounds, the plainness of which does not even hint at the unspeakable acts that created them." In parallel language, he illustrates their lack of hope: "Here they lie, never to hope, never to pray, never to love, never to heal, never to laugh, never to cry."

But, again, he cannot give into this hopeless situation. He offers hope, even in this place of death and suffering, and resumes his role as secular pastor: "And too many of them knew that this was their fate, but that was not the end. Through it all was their faith and a spirit that moved their faith." That spirit and faith are illustrated in the story of one person. This next section of the speech is typical of most Reagan speeches. He chooses one person to personify all those who suffered at Bergen-Belsen. He tells the emotional story of that person, a story that supports his theme, and then he draws a lesson for the audience. Often the person chosen for the story is not well known, but in this case he uses the story of Anne Frank: "Nothing illustrates this better than the story of a young girl who died here at Bergen-Belsen. For more than two years Anne Frank and her family had hidden from the Nazis in a confined annex in Holland where she kept a remarkably profound diary. Betrayed by an informant, Anne and her family were sent by freight car first to Auschwitz and finally here to Bergen-Belsen."

Even though she died at Bergen-Belsen, Reagan uses Anne Frank's words as a testament to the goodness of people and the hope of a better world, and in many respects Anne Frank's words reflect many of Ronald Reagan's personal beliefs: "Just three weeks before her capture, young Anne wrote these words: 'It's really a wonder that I haven't dropped all my ideals because they seem so absurd and impossible to carry out. Yet I keep them because in spite of everything I still believe that people are good at heart. I simply can't build up my hopes on a foundation consisting of confusion, misery, and death. I see the world gradually being turned into a wilderness. I hear the ever approaching thunder which will destroy us too; I can feel the suffering of millions and yet, if I looked up into the heavens I think that it will all come out right, that this cruelty will and that peace and tranquility will return again.'" In contrast to the hopefulness in her words, Reagan adds, "Eight months later, this sparkling young life ended here at Bergen-Belsen." He punctuates his words with this brief exclamation: "Somewhere here lies Anne Frank." That brief sentence emphasizes the horrors of a system that would destroy the hopes of vibrant young people like Anne Frank.

In choosing Anne Frank as a symbol of the Holocaust, Reagan again opened himself to criticism from his critics, who argued that this emphasis downplayed the sacrifice of millions of others who died in the camps. The story of Anne Frank is powerful and adds feeling to his message. It did little, however, to endear him to critics who felt that he did not understand them and their suffering or to overcome the hard feelings of previous weeks.

After telling the story of Anne Frank, Reagan moves to the lesson to be learned from his message: Even out of suffering and dying in concentration camps, Reagan believes there will be healing and redemption. As a secular preacher, he tells his audience that the lives of all people can make the world a better place: "Everywhere here there are memories—pulling us, touching us, making us understand that they can never be erased. Such memories take us where God intended His children to go—toward learning, toward healing, and, above all, toward redemption. They beckon us through the endless sketches of our heart to the knowing commitment that the life of each individual can change the world and make it better." He almost seems to be saying that only through suffering and death can healing and redemption occur—that the deaths of World War II were necessary to lead to the reconciliation of nations in the 1980s and the achievement of a better world. This is a natural expression of Reagan's spirit of optimism but one that would be difficult for many to accept, especially those who suffered in World War II while Reagan was living at home and making movies in Culver City, California.

Reagan's conclusion reiterates his hope for truth, and he quotes Abraham Lincoln's first inaugural address: "We're all witnesses; we share the glistening hope that rests in every human soul. Hope leads us, if we're prepared to trust it, toward what our President Lincoln called the better angels of our nature. And then rising above all this cruelty, out of this tragic and nightmarish time, beyond the anguish, the pain and suffering for all time, we must pledge: Never again."[9] He had uttered these same words many times during the controversy over his visit to Germany, and they did not seem to calm his critics or convince them that he really did care for Jewish survivors of the Holocaust. Reagan could only hope that this time they believed him and accepted his words.

Bernard Weinraub describes Reagan standing before the obelisk, "his voice low and drained" as he gave his speech.[10] Morris, in describing the scene, said that Reagan spoke "hoarsely to a small group of German and American dignitaries. They sat facing him on six rows of damp folding chairs, their backs to a thousand-acre field edged with spruce and white birch. Its heathery surface, dull green under the dull North German sky, rose flatly over long, low earthen barrows, unmarked except for tablets that recorded the number of bodies buried in each." His description goes on to include the reaction of the audience: "He was listened to in absolute silence. His every sigh was audible in the misty air, as was the surrounding rustle of the woods. Unnecessary loudspeakers brayed his words across the emptiness of the Bergen field. Not so much as a cornerstone broke the smoothness of grass and heather: the camp had proved so pestilential on liberation that British soldiers had burned it to the ground."[11]

According to Morris, Reagan was able to maintain control of his emotions until he began to talk about the death of children in the camp:

His voice growled on each verb, and he fought tears through a peroration on the camp's most famous victim, Anne Frank. For the only line that stopped him came from Anne Frank: "In spite of everything I still believe that people are really good at heart." The rawness of his delivery was threatened ultimately by sentimental evocations of hearts and angels and glistening hopes. But he held himself stiffly to the end, and Leonard Bernstein could not have better timed his agogic beat before, "Never again." There was no applause. He shuffled his cards, tried and failed to find a pocket to put them in. The wet breeze whipped his coat. Then, with eyes still downcast, he stepped off the monument, leaving a wreath of green ferns behind him. The silence lasted until he found his seat.[12]

After his speech, Reagan placed a wreath near an obelisk, and he and the Kohls left for Bitburg.

Later, Reagan described his visit to Bergen-Belsen: "This was an emotional experience. We went through the small museum with the enlarged photos of the horrors there. Then we walked past the mounds planted with heather each being a mass grave for 5000 or more of the people, largely Jews but also many Christians who had been slaughtered there or who were just starved to death." He then addressed the importance of his speaking during the visit: "Here I made the speech I hoped would refute the phony charges that had been made. I declared that we must *not* forget and we must pledge 'never again.' Before the day was out there were reports that my talk had been effective."[13] Perhaps his natural optimism would not allow him to think that he had gone through such a draining emotional experience without calming the emotions that had surfaced during the conflict.

Time described the speech as "a skillful exercise in both the art of eulogy and political damage control."[14] Observers were not in agreement as to whether he succeeded in controlling the damage.

Cannon describes what he believes was the importance of the speech at Bergen-Belsen: "What Reagan said at Bergen-Belsen meant more than his silent participation in the ceremony at the Bitburg cemetery." The speech "would prove the last great commemorative speech of his presidency." Reagan would take many future trips and give many speeches in foreign countries, "but while Reagan wandered down memory lane on many of these occasions, his most stirring speeches looked to the future of the new era in East-West relations rather than to the past." For Cannon, Mikhail Gorbachev had become the dominant figure in the world, and Reagan was overshadowed by him for the rest of his presidency.[15]

After Reagan and Kohl left Bergen-Belsen, "rows of invited guests, shaking hands and chatting, then filed out and climbed into the Mercedes-Benz limousines of postwar West German prosperity." About twenty minutes later, a group of Jews, "some former inmates and some the children of victims, entered the concentration camp in a somber procession, each bearing a rose and many in tears." They held a service to "reconsecrate" the site because Reagan and Kohl had "desecrated" the camp. They were angry that only invited guests were allowed inside the camp during the ceremony and demonstrators were restricted access to the site. The leader of the ceremony said, "Today, we say to them that they can either honor the memory of the victims of Belsen, or they can honor the SS. They cannot do both."[16] Obviously, many of Reagan's critics were not willing to accept what he said in the speech or forgive him for the act of visiting a cemetery that contained the remains of soldiers who had tortured and murdered prisoners in the camps.

The Speech at Bitburg

The next stop was the military cemetery at Bitburg that initially caused the controversy. Reagan had to deliver one more speech, but the most difficult and emotional one of the day was completed. He now moved to a more supportive audience. Reagan and Kohl were greeted at the air base by thousands of people who waived American and German flags. They rode in a limousine to the cemetery. Outside the cemetery there were groups of demonstrators, but they were kept a significant distance away and so had little effect on the event.[17] Reagan would hardly have been aware of their presence.

Their visit to the cemetery was solemn: "As the two leaders walked slowly past the graves, West German Army musicians played a somber drum roll. Mr. Reagan and Mr. Kohl briefly arranged two large circular wreaths at the foot of the memorial tower before standing to attention. For several moments silence fell across the cemetery, except for the click of cameras. A trumpeter played a melancholy German soldiers' song, 'I Had a Comrade.' The song mourns fallen soldiers."[18] Reagan met families of German resistance leaders and spoke to Gen. Matthew Ridgway, a commander of U.S. forces in World War II who volunteered to accompany Reagan to the ceremonies. General Ridgway had been quoted a year earlier in Reagan's speech at Pointe du Hoc, and Reagan was happy to have his support during the difficult visit to the cemetery.

"Accompanied by Chancellor Helmut Kohl, Mr. Reagan walked slowly through the narrow, hilltop cemetery, ablaze with tulips and marigolds. Mr. Reagan did not glance at the graves during his eight min-ute visit."[19] The criticism Reagan had received had a significant effect on the itinerary for the trip. The visit to the cemetery was downplayed and almost became an afterthought. This was a change from Reagan's trip a year earlier to Normandy, where he spent a significant amount of time walking among the graves. Reagan and his aides wanted visuals from Normandy seen on television and elsewhere. The opposite was true at Bitburg. According to Richard Reeves, "The path Reagan and Kohl took through the cemetery was anti-Deaverish planned by Deaver himself. Usually, he choreographed camera angles to show Reagan at work, but this time the faces of the President and the Chancellor were hidden behind trees and hedges."[20] They wanted little such attention to his journey to the cemetery, and they had no desire to use the visuals from the trip in future Reagan speeches or television ads. They wanted the event over and behind them.

An editorial in the *Washington Post* points to an irony in Reagan's visit. Reagan had argued that he could "not afford to back off the trip to Bitburg because to do so would make him look weak, a man suscep-tible to pressures, to being pushed around." But Reagan did look weak at Bitburg: "The Ronald Reagan who walked stiffly into the cemetery and out again with Chancellor Helmut Kohl seemed almost robot-like, *led*. Our president was in that eight minutes forever being cued, nudged, positioned—stage-managed—by the chancellor. He exuded not wanting to be there. It was not an image of mastery."[21]

Morris describes the visit to Bitburg as anticlimactic. "In eight word-less minutes, they perambulated the tiny cemetery, fingered rather than laid wreaths at the Wehrmacht memorial, allowed Generals Matthew Ridgway and Johannes Steinhoff, a decorated German veteran of World War II, to shake hands in their stead, then left without looking at any graves. Kohl used a large handkerchief to brush tears from his face."[22]

For Cannon, the speech at Bergen-Belsen had "alleviated the ignominy of Bitburg. . . . It was a striking example, of which there have been many in Reagan's life, where he was rescued from poor judgment by a successful performance. And Reagan's discomfort was also eased by the participation of ninety-years-old General Matthew Ridgway, who had led the U.S. 82nd Airborne Division in the war against Nazi Germany and who volunteered to lay the wreath with Reagan at the Bitburg cemetery. While Ridgway's participation did not dim the criticism of the president's actions, it made the ceremony easier for Reagan to endure."[23] Ridgway also became a symbol that Reagan could effectively use in his speech to emphasize that former enemies were now allies and friends.

In his diary Reagan, describes people jamming the streets. Most were friendly but some were demonstrators. At the cemetery he met General Ridgway, the last surviving major U.S. leader of World War II, and General Steinhoff, "who had been shot down in flames and whose face had been rebuilt by an American army doctor at war's end." Reagan, Kohl, and the generals walked through the cemetery, and the generals placed wreaths at a monument. Reagan then described an emotional moment: "The German 'Taps' was played and then in a truly dramatic moment, the two generals clasped hands."[24] That gesture supported Reagan's statement of the progress in the relationship between Americans and Germans since the end of World War II.

After the visit to the cemetery, the participants drove to the U.S. base near Bitburg, where Kohl and Reagan again spoke. The situation here was not as tense, and the leaders were in front of an audience that viewed them favorably.

Kohl's speech was longer than the one at Bergen-Belsen, and he seemed more at ease here.[25] He began by echoing Reagan's theme for the day, the meeting of past and present: "It is not often that the link between the past, present and future of our country reaches us as vividly as during these hours at Bitburg." He referred to the visit to the cemetery and the emotion it caused: "Our visit to the soldiers' graves here in Bitburg was not an easy one. It could not but arouse deep feelings. For me it meant first and foremost deep sorrow and grief at the infinite suffering that the war and totalitarianism inflicted on nations, sorrow and grief that will never cease." He then reiterated that the trip was a reaffirmation of the reconciliation between the United States and Germany. He thanked Reagan for his visit, even though it had caused a great deal of anguish in both nations: "I thank you Mr. President, both on behalf of the whole German people, and I thank you very personally as a friend, for visiting the graves with me. I believe that many of our German people understand this expression of deep friendship, and that it presages a good future for our nations." Reagan had endured a great deal of criticism because of his visit to Bitburg at Kohl's request. It would be appropriate for Kohl to thank him for his loyalty.

The rest of the speech outlined the importance of places like Bitburg, where both German and U.S. military personnel were stationed. Kohl spoke to the German soldiers and told them how fortunate they were to have not taken part in World War II and only gotten to know Americans "as helpers, as partners and allies," not as enemies in combat. He thanked the U.S. troops for their sacrifice in serving in Germany and told them that their presence was vital to the security of West Germany. He noted that the cooperation between the two military forces "strengthens our joint determination to defend the peace and freedom of our nations" and is "a source of mutual understanding of our people, generating many personal friendships." He concluded, "I wish the members of the U.S. forces, I wish our soldiers of the Federal Armed Forces, I wish for us all that together we make our contribution to the peace and freedom of our country and of the world—and may God's blessing be with us." These words would seem to indicate that Kohl was confident that Reagan could be counted on to support him in any conflict that he might have with the Soviet Union or other totalitarian states.

Reagan and his staff hoped his appearance at Bergen-Belsen and his emotional speech there had reduced the negative feelings of the day. His audience at Bitburg was composed mainly of people who would view him positively, so he could feel more comfortable than at the anguish-filled concentration camp or cemetery. His speech is much longer here, but it repeats many of the same themes: the bitter condemnation of the Nazis and the suffering caused by World War II balanced by the reconciliation and hope during the forty years since the war ended. As in the earlier speech, he uses stories and examples of remarkable individual lives to support his message and lessons, but those lives were not of famous people like Anne Frank. The speech is vintage Ronald Reagan.

Reagan begins this speech less formally than the speech at Bergen-Belsen.[26] He does not acknowledge Kohl and the other guests but states simply, "Thank you very much." He begins by immediately focusing on the issue of his visit to the cemetery. He would be compelled by the situation to acknowledge the place that had caused him so much frustration. Even though he was at the cemetery only briefly, Reagan describes the emotions he felt. He begins by speaking in first person, something he did not do at any length in the Bergen-Belsen speech but seems to do extensively in this speech. The use of first person may have been an attempt to personalize the occasion, to illustrate his individual feelings: "I have just come from the cemetery where German war dead lay at rest." He makes it clear at the beginning that the cemetery contains only German soldiers. This simple statement acknowledges the concern of World War II veterans that he was not visiting a cemetery that contained Americans killed in the war. He continues, "No one could visit there without deep and conflicting emotions. I felt sadness that history could be filled with such waste, destruction, and evil, but my heart was also lifted by the knowledge that from the ashes has come hope and from the terrors of the past we have built 40 years of peace, freedom, and reconciliation among nations." He returns to the powerful image of hope emerging from the ashes of the past. There is one quite dramatic difference between the two speeches at this early point. At Bergen-Belsen the language was made harsh and vivid with powerful adjectives. At Bitburg, Reagan describes suffering but with words like "waste," "destruction," and "evil" but not with adjectives that make the imagery even more dramatic. This image of hope rising from ashes again reflects his natural sense of optimism that goodness can come out of the most evil of situations and again serves as one of the major themes of the day.

Reagan reaches out to his critics, particularly American veterans and survivors of the Holocaust, in the hope of reconciliation. He openly acknowledges the disagreements and conflicts of the previous weeks. He continues to speak in first person: "This visit has stirred many emotions in the American and German people, too. I've received many letters since first deciding to come to Bitburg Cemetery; some supportive, others deeply concerned and questioning, and others opposed. Some old wounds have been reopened, and this I regret very much because this should be a time of healing." Throughout his presidency Reagan was very interested in the messages he had received in letters, so he was aware of what was being said to him by those who took the time to write. He uses this speech in his attempt to heal the wounds of the previous weeks. The Great Communicator must again use words to extract himself from a difficult situation and to heal the wounds opened by the controversy. At the end of the speech, Reagan talks of healing suffering and pain. Early in the speech he must try to heal the wounds caused by the controversy, so healing is an important theme throughout the speech.

He first addresses American veterans and their families. He had not spoken directly to veterans at length at Bergen-Belsen, so he tries to respond to their concerns in this speech. Reagan speechwriter Josh Gilder argues that the very fact that Reagan was speaking at a military base would serve as a form of honoring of veterans.[27]

Veterans had traditionally been strong supporters of Reagan, but many were upset because he visited a German cemetery and not one that contained the remains of American soldiers: "To the veterans and families of American servicemen who still carry the scars and feel the painful losses of that war, our gesture of reconciliation with the German people in no way minimizes our love and honor for those who fought and died for our country. They gave their lives to rescue freedom in its darkest hours." He does not dwell on the sorrow surrounding the loss of life but talks about how those soldiers' sacrifice made the world a better place: "The alliance of democratic nations that guards the freedom of millions in Europe and America today stands as living testament that their noble sacrifice was not in vain." Thus he links the effort by World War II veterans to fight Nazis with the current battle with the Soviet Union and other enemies. He adds emphasis by repeating, "No, their sacrifice was not in vain." This short sentence punctuates and stresses the meaning of the longer passages before it. Reagan had used a similar tactic at Bergen-Belsen.

To support his point that the loss of life in World War II was not in vain, Reagan tells a brief story and points to two individuals who had reconciled at Bitburg cemetery, two officers who had fought on opposing sides of the war: "I have to tell you that nothing will ever fill me with greater hope than the sight of two former war heroes who met today at the Bitburg ceremony; each among the bravest of the brave; each an enemy of the other 40 years ago; each a witness to the horrors of war. But today they came together, American and German, General Matthew B. Ridgway and General Johannes Steinhoff, reconciled and united for freedom. They reached over the graves to one another like brothers and grasped their hands in peace." At the height of the controversy over Bitburg, General Ridgway had called Reagan and offered to do whatever he could to help. Reagan was not aware that Ridgway was still alive, but he quickly accepted Ridgway's offer and asked him to make the trip to Europe. Ridgway became a symbol that Reagan could use to support the arguments in his speech: one of the few remaining leaders of World War II accepting reconciliation with a leader of his former enemies. Reagan did not have to say it, but if General Ridgway could reconcile with his foe, then all people should be able to come together in peace.

He next spoke directly to the survivors of the Holocaust. He had spent a considerable amount of time and effort in the speech at Bergen-Belsen appealing to the survivors, trying to describe their suffering, assuring them that others felt their pain, and telling them that the world had not forgotten the horrors they had endured. He now reiterated that the United States and its president would not forget them: "Your terrible suffering has made you ever vigilant against evil. Many of you are worried that reconciliation means forgetting. Well, I promise you, we will never forget." As a reminder, he points to his visit earlier that day: "I have just come this morning from Bergen-Belsen, where the horror of that terrible crime, the Holocaust, was forever burned upon my memory. No we will never forget, and we say with the victims of that Holocaust: Never again." He had used this line numerous times during the controversy, and he hoped that its use this time and in this place would make it clear to the survivors that he meant what he said.

Having reached out to the veterans of World War II and to the survivors of the Holocaust, Reagan confronts the conflict over the soldiers buried in the Bitburg cemetery. His comments probably did not ease the concerns of many of the Holocaust survivors he had just mentioned. He begins by condemning Hitler but does not use Hitler's name: "The war against one man's totalitarian dictatorship was not like other wars. The evil war of Nazism turned all values upside down." His description of the war and the actions of one evil dictator as being unique in history allows him the opportunity to speak of the dead German soldiers in different terms: "Nevertheless, we can mourn the German war dead today as human beings crushed by a vicious ideology." In some respects, the soldiers are victims of the war, much the same as the Holocaust survivors. This inference was the very one that brought Reagan so much criticism in the weeks before the trip to Germany. It also reiterates the interpretation of history he outlined in the speech at Bergen-Belsen, an interpretation that many of his critics rejected.

During the weeks before the trip, Reagan's aides attempted to learn as much as they could about the lives of the soldiers buried in Bitburg cemetery. There was serious consideration of using the story of individual soldiers to support the arguments in Reagan's speech, but the decision was eventually made to simply refer to them as a group. In the speech Reagan states that there were more than two thousand soldiers buried in the cemetery and then focuses on the specific soldiers who caused the controversy: "Among them are 48 members of the SS—the

crimes of the SS must rank among the most heinous in human history."
He then contrasts those criminals with the majority of the dead: "But
others buried there were simply soldiers in the German Army." Rather
than make specific comments about individuals, he asks a series of
questions that cannot really be answered: "How many were fanatical
followers of a dictator and willfully carried out his cruel orders? And
how many were conscripts, forced into service during the death throes
of the Nazi war machine?" He answers his own questions, but in a way
that seems to imply that most of them were unwilling conscripts forced
into fighting for a lost cause: "We do not know. Many, however, we know
from the dates on their tombstones, were only teenagers at the time.
There is one boy buried there who died a week before his 16th birthday."
Although Reagan knows the soldier's name, rather than refer to him
by name he makes him the symbol of all German soldiers who died
a needless death in a war created by Hitler and his Nazi followers. He
implies that these soldiers could not be condemned in the same way as
the SS troops. Again, as at Bergen-Belsen, he focuses on the death of a
young person, seeming to say that the death of one so young was even
worse that the death of older people. He then continues on the same
theme: "There were thousands of such soldiers to whom Nazism meant
no more than a brutal end to a short life." These soldiers could not be
condemned for the actions of the very small minority, the members
of the dreaded SS.

Reagan again proposes the historical interpretation that the events of
World War II were caused by one man and his fanatical followers, not
by a majority of Germans. Hitler and the other Nazi leaders should be
condemned, but not all Germans could be blamed: "We do not believe
in collective guilt." He had used those words in the weeks leading to
the Bitburg visit. Those who did not accept this view of history would
be upset by the remark.

He now assumes his role of secular preacher and answers those
critics with another comment used many times in the weeks before
Bitburg: "Only God can look into the human heart, and all these men
have now met their supreme judge, and they have been judged by Him
as we shall all be judged." Reagan, speaking as a pastor to the world,

seems to say that it is not the role of humans to judge, but in the end all must be judged by God. Many of his critics did not accept this view and believed that many, if not all Germans, must share blame for the events in World War II.

The speech seems divided into two parts, just like the one at Bergen-Belsen. Until this point in the speech, Reagan seems to be speaking of the past and the evil that occurred in the past. Now he moves from a judgment of evil to hope and the goodness present even in the most evil of situations. His natural sense of optimism returns: "Our duty today is to mourn the human wreckage of totalitarianism, and today in Bitburg cemetery we commemorated the potential good in humanity that was consumed back then, 40 years ago." He returns to the young soldier mentioned earlier and to the potential that all young people have: "Perhaps if that 15-year-old soldier had lived, he would have joined his fellow countrymen in building this new democratic Federal Republic of Germany, devoted to human dignity and the defense of freedom we celebrate today. Or perhaps his children or his grandchildren might be among you here today at the Bitburg Air Base, where new generations of Germans and Americans join together in friendship and common cause, dedicating their lives to preserving peace and guarding the security of the free world." The implication is quite clear: Given a choice, individuals like that young soldier would work for good and for understanding rather than serve tyrants and commit the horrible crimes of World War II. The statement shows Reagan at his most optimistic, and his words reflect the belief that people are basically good and moral.

In keeping with his optimistic view, Reagan returns to a statement he used in the weeks leading up to the speeches to show that the reconciliation among nations after World War II is unique in history: "Too often in the past each war only planted the seeds of the next. We celebrate today the reconciliation between our two nations that has liberated us from that cycle of destruction." He makes the achievements concrete in the use of parallel language: "Look at what together we've accomplished. We who were enemies are now friends; we who were bitter adversaries are now the strongest of allies. In the place of fear we've sown trust, and out of the ruins of war has blossomed an enduring peace." This expression can be linked to the theme of spring and rebirth and to the image that he had also used at Bergen-Belsen. It also illustrates how much of the speech was really a summation of the arguments he had been making in defending his position before the trip to Germany.

Reagan uses the Bitburg community and the military base as concrete evidence of the success of the reconciliation. His staff had carefully researched the history of the base at Bitburg, so he was able to use concrete words and numbers in this section of the speech: "Tens of thousands of Americans have served in this town over the years. As the mayor of Bitburg has said, in that time there have been some 6,000 marriages between Germans and Americans, and many thousands of children have come from these unions." The research even included personal information about the mayor in case Reagan wished to speak of him by name or to list his accomplishments. After describing the great achievements of the past, Reagan turns to an even more successful future, a future based on his optimistic worldview: "This is the real symbol of our future together, a future to be filled with hope, friendship, and freedom." These were the same words used to describe the future in the Bergen-Belsen speech.

To further express his optimistic view of the world and the hope of cooperation between former enemies, Reagan uses his typical strategy of telling a story that contains a moral message. The story is emotional and makes up a significant amount of the speech. He begins in an optimistic vein: "The hope that we now see could sometimes even be glimpsed in the darkest days of the war. I'm thinking of one special story—that of a mother and her young son living alone in a modest cottage in the middle of the war." The event takes place during the Battle of the Bulge, one of the last great battles of the war. One night as the battle "exploded not far away, and around them, three young soldiers arrived at their door—they were standing there in the snow, lost behind enemy lines. All were frostbitten; one was badly wounded. Even though sheltering the enemy was punishable by death, she took them in and made them a supper with some of her last food." Her problems were compounded when she heard another knock on the door and opened it to discover four German soldiers: "The woman was afraid, but she quickly said with a firm voice, 'There will be no shooting here.'" The soldiers laid down their weapons and joined in the meal: "Heinz and Willi, it turned out, were only 16; the corporal was the oldest at 23. Their natural suspicion dissolved in the warmth and comfort of the cottage. One of the Germans, a former medical student, tended the wounded American." Again, the youth of the soldiers is stressed, particularly the ones who were "only 16." Gilder sees this emphasis on youth in both of the speeches as classic Reagan, a theme he used in many speeches throughout his career.[28]

Reagan tells the story from the viewpoint of the young son: "'The mother said grace. I noticed that there were tears in her eyes as she said the old, familiar words, Komm, Herr Jesus. Be our guest. And as I looked around the table, I saw tears, too, in the eyes of the battle-weary soldiers, boys again, some from America, some from Germany, all far from home.'"

The soldiers passed the stormy night in "their own private armistice." The next morning, "the German corporal showed the Americans how to get back behind their own lines. And they all shook hands and went their separate ways." The story is emotional, and Reagan makes it even more powerful by punctuating it with one final line: "That happened to be Christmas Day, 40 years ago." Now Reagan returns to his role as secular preacher and states the lesson that can be learned from the story: "Those boys reconciled briefly in the midst of war. Surely we allies in peacetime should honor the reconciliation of the last 40 years." He then acknowledges that same hospitality in the present: "To the people of Bitburg, our hosts and the hosts of our servicemen, like that generous woman 40 years ago, you make us feel very welcome. Vielen dank. [Many thanks.]"

This story was published many years after the events in *Reader's Digest,* one of Reagan's favorite magazines and one of his main sources of information for speeches throughout his career. The author of the published story was the young boy and narrator mentioned above. In the Reagan Library is a copy of a memo from the *Reader's Digest* that describes the extensive length the magazine went to verify the account in the story. The editors thought that the story was compelling, but they wanted to make sure the events were real. The person who did the research concluded that the story was true, and the magazine published it.[29]

Many of Reagan's critics questioned his reliance on sources like *Reader's Digest*. The use of a story from that publication would raise the issue of Reagan's lack of intellect and lack of a sense of history. From a rhetorical point of view, however, this war story was powerful and just the kind of story someone as adept as Reagan at telling stories could use effectively.

Reagan now thanks the men and women stationed at Bitburg and praises them for their service: "I just want to say that we know that even with such wonderful hosts, your job is not an easy one. You serve around the clock far from home, always ready to defend freedom. We're grateful, and we're very proud of you."

After thanking the members of the military, he returns to the lessons learned from World War II: "Four decades ago we waged a great war to lift the darkness of evil from the world, to let men and women in this country and in every country live in the sunshine of liberty." This sentence introduces a theme heard throughout the final third of the speech: the balancing of dark and light images. The dark images stand for evil and hate, the light images for hope or for freeing people from evil and hate.[30]

Even though the nations that fought in World War II have emerged into the light, Reagan says, there are still many places in the world that remain in darkness. He now moves to the part of the speech that, according to Gilder, is most important—where he asks his audience to change from a focus on the evils of the Nazis to the evils of the current tyrants in the world: "Our victory was great, and the Federal Republic, Italy, and Japan are in the community of free nations. But the struggle for freedom is not complete, for much of the world is still cast in totalitarian darkness." This is a not too subtle attack on the Soviet Union and its allies, one of Reagan's traditional targets. Reagan is reminding his audience that free people must be ever vigilant in opposing totalitarianism. It is fitting that the message should be delivered on a U.S.

military base with a primary purpose of opposing the Soviet Union and its allies.

Reagan proposes that a means of bringing those in darkness into the light is for all free people to identify with those living under dictators. Reagan begins this section by speaking of John F. Kennedy and his famous speech in Berlin in 1962: "Twenty-two years ago President John F. Kennedy went to the Berlin Wall and proclaimed that he, too, was a Berliner."[31] Germans would remember Kennedy's speech and the sentiments it expressed fondly. Reagan extends Kennedy's words to many parts of the world where people are fighting for freedom, using a series of parallel statements to achieve his goal: "Today, freedom-loving people around the world must say: I am a Berliner. I am a Jew in a world still threatened by anti-Semitism. I am an Afghan, and I am a prisoner of the Gulag. I am a refugee in a crowded boat floundering off the coast of Vietnam. I am a Laotian, a Cambodian, a Cuban, and a Miskito Indian in Nicaragua. Everyone must say, I, too, am a potential victim of totalitarianism." He asks his audience to become one with all those who are oppressed. If the free people of the world can come together, they will defeat totalitarianism and the evil dictators of the world.

Reagan now turns to a theme discussed throughout his presidency: the need for the United States and other nations to be strong militarily in order to oppose dictatorial regimes throughout the world. He is not specific in his proposals, but this section can be seen as a call for Europeans and Americans to remain vigilant in opposition to communism: "The one lesson of World War II, the one lesson of Nazism, is that freedom must always be stronger than totalitarianism and that good must be stronger than evil. The moral measure of our two nations will be found in the resolve that we show to preserve liberty, to protect life, and to honor and cherish all God's children." He uses West Germany as an illustration of a nation that has chosen good over evil: "That is why the free, democratic Federal Republic of Germany is such a profound and hopeful testament to the human spirit." This is also a call to Chancellor Kohl to remain steady in the face of the many enemies of freedom.

Reagan tempers his hope and calls upon those listening to use the lessons of the past to build a better future: "We cannot undo the crimes and wars of yesterday nor call the millions back to life, but we can give meaning to the past by learning its lessons and making a better future. We can let our pain drive us to greater efforts to heal humanity's suffering." That pain could only be eased by defeating the enemies of freedom.

He reflects on the events of the day and the conflict of the past weeks. In talking about his day, he uses imagery that balances the past and the future and reintroduces the images of light: "Today I've traveled 220 miles from Bergen-Belsen and, I feel, 40 years in time. With the lessons of the past firmly in our minds, we've turned a new, brighter page in history."

He closes the discussion of the criticism he received during previous weeks by referring to a letter he received from a young Jewish girl who supports his visit to Bitburg: "One of the many who wrote me about this visit was a young woman who had recently been bas mitzvahed. She urged me to lay the wreath at Bitburg cemetery in honor of the future of Germany. And that is what we have done."[32] He uses the letter and its young author to symbolize all who supported his visit and also as a confirmation that he had indeed done the right thing by visiting the cemetery.

Once Reagan has confirmed that his actions are correct, he repeats the purpose of his visit, the commemoration of the fortieth anniversary of the end of World War II in Europe, and illustrates the importance of the day by balancing opposites—the evil of oppression and the rebirth of democracy: "On this 40th anniversary of World War II, we mark the day when the hate, the evil, and the obscenities ended, and we commemorate the rekindling of the democratic spirit in Germany."

Reagan felt that one of the great symbols of reconciliation and hope was a German band playing the American national anthem and an American band playing the German national anthem before the speech. He builds on that image by once again balancing images of dark and light: "While much of the world still huddles in the darkness of oppression we can see a new dawn of freedom sweeping the globe. And we can see in the new democracies of Latin America, in the new economic freedoms and prosperity in Asia, in the slow movement toward peace in the Middle East, and in the strengthening alliance of democratic nations in Europe and America that the light from that dawn is growing stronger." He carries that image through one last statement: "Together, let us gather in that light and walk out of the shadow. Let us live in peace."

He concludes in typical fashion: "Thank you, and God bless you all."

Later, Reagan evaluated his speech at Bitburg: "My speech was sort of a sequel to the one at Belsen. It was enthusiastically received and our people thought it turned the issue around. I felt very good. I was told later the two generals sat holding each other's hands." He concluded that the day had been a great success: "Well, this was the day—everyone—well, not everyone—but much of the press had predicted would be a disaster."[33] At the end of the day, he could not bring himself to admit that perhaps the speeches had not been as successful as he hoped.

Reagan concluded the chapter of his book on Bitburg with the following assessment: "I have never regretted not canceling the trip to Bitburg. In the end, I believe my visit to the cemetery and the dramatic and unexpected gesture by two old soldiers from opposing sides of the battlefield helped strengthen our European alliance and heal once and for all many of the lingering wounds of the war."[34] This comment provides some evidence that his goal was to strengthen the alliance in opposition to the Soviet Union as well as to commemorate the end of World War II.

Memorials as Rhetoric

Reagan's trip to Bergen-Belsen and Bitburg illustrates the power of visits to memorials honoring the dead. James Young proposes that "the creators of memorial texts necessarily reconstruct historical events, and so reflect as much their own understanding and experiences as the actual events they would preserve." He further states that "*what* is remembered here necessarily depends on *how* it is remembered; and how these events are remembered depends in turn on the icons that do the remembering." As he says, "A nation's monuments efface as much history as they inscribe on it." He concludes that the aim of monuments "is not solely to displace memory or to remake it in one's own image; it is also to invite the collaboration of the community in acts of remembrance."³⁵

The meaning of the memorials at Bergen-Belsen and Bitburg was open to numerous interpretations, and they were remembered in different ways by those who viewed them. Holocaust survivors, veterans who fought in World War II and their families, and Ronald Reagan viewed those memorials from different limited perspectives. Each created an interpretation of history based on their perceptions and each was part of a community of remembrance. Reagan used these ceremonial situations in an attempt to create a community that accepted his interpretation of events surrounding the memorials. He relied on myths he hoped would be acceptable to all members of the community. It was unlikely that members of all groups could or would accept his interpretation, but he had to make such an effort if his speeches were to be successful.

Rhetorical scholar Marouf Hasian focuses his study of memorials on the Bergen-Belsen concentration camp site. He agrees with Young when he states, "As new generations visit memorials, take tours, watch videos, or hear about archeological discoveries, they are being invited to participate in symbolic acts of selective remembering and forgetting."³⁶ Hasian illustrates his point by examining the evolution of the image of Bergen-Belsen and its most famous internee, Anne Frank, from the end of World War II until the present.

The camp at Bergen-Belsen was liberated by the British on April 15, 1945. The soldiers found thousands of prisoners in the middle of a typhus epidemic. Just before the arrival of the British, both Anne Frank and her sister Margot had died. Hasian quotes Raymond Phillips's description of the camp: "Belsen became the symbol of all that had been told (and scarcely credited) of the vileness and rottenness of the Nazi system. Other camps were unearthed as the Allied Armies moved forward, and some of them were worse than Belsen, at least with regard to their calculated savagery and cruelty. But Belsen, because it was the first of which an impartial account was available, became the archetype of the rest; and a proof that it was not an imaginary evil which the Allies had been fighting for almost six years. With public horror at the stories that came from Belsen went a public demand that those responsible should be punished for the deeds." After the war, in the "Belsen trials," camp commander Josef Kramer and forty-four other Germans were charged with war crimes. Kramer and several officers were hanged and others received long prison terms.[37]

Hasian describes the changes of the image of the camp over the years. For several years after the trials there was little mention of the camp or its victims. The world seemed to need a time of healing, a time to forget the horrors of World War II. The memory of the camp was kept alive by the stories of survivors who organized groups like the World Federation of Bergen-Belsen Associations. These people "were simply not interested in perpetuating the individuated memory of popular icons like Anne Frank." Rather, "they celebrated the material and symbolic 'rebirth' of the community that had survived the camps." But the publication of the diary of Anne Frank and the plays and movie based on the diary appealed to Europeans' interest "in messages of rebirth, regeneration, and reconciliation. Audiences that might have ignored the Allied postwar trials could identify with figures like Anne Frank." By the end of the 1950s, Bergen-Belsen "was going to be remembered as the final resting place of Anne Frank";[38] in the late 1960s and early 1970s, Anne Frank became a universal symbol "of all those who were and still are persecuted innocently because of race, belief or color";[39] and by the 1980s there were competing arguments of the nature of the Holocaust: "Some scholars and lay persons were still worried that not enough time and effort had been spent on remembering specific events associated with the Holocaust, while others responded that this was a time for forgetting and reconciliation."[40]

Hasian then turns specifically to Reagan's visit to Bergen-Belsen. He proposes that Reagan, in his visit to Bergen-Belsen and Bitburg, argued that 1985 was a time for reconciliation, not recrimination. Reagan also chose to use Anne Frank as a universal symbol of the Holocaust. But Reagan's decision to use Anne Frank as a symbol was not acceptable to his opponents: "The president's visits to both Bitburg and Bergen-Belsen did not please everyone, and his reconciliation theme did not sit well with observers who worried that such declamations were trivializing the horrors of the Holocaust."[41]

Hasian situates Reagan's visit as part of a long battle over the meaning of the powerful memorial at Bergen-Belsen—a battle full of great emotion because of the power of Bergen-Belsen as a symbol, a symbol viewed differently by different groups. Hasian also illustrates the problems Reagan would face in confronting the legacy of Bergen-Belsen in his speech.

CHAPTER 5

A Seminal Symbolic Disaster:
Reagan at Bitburg, May 5, 1985

After his triumphant speeches at the fortieth anniversary of the D-Day invasion in 1984, Ronald Reagan seemed to become more comfortable speaking in ceremonial settings in Europe. His well-written and well-delivered speeches took place in locations chosen for the maximum visual effects for television and other media. The speeches were delivered when they would receive maximum attention on television in the United States and, in many respects, they were written and delivered for an audience in the United States even though they were presented in Europe. The speeches were so effective that they were used in television commercials during Reagan's reelection campaign that year.

Reagan's return to Europe the following year for the celebration of the end of World War II was not as successful. Although his speechwriters had prepared two carefully crafted speeches, the controversy surrounding the speeches made it difficult, if not impossible, for him to repeat his successes and to receive the kind of acclaim he had received after the speeches at Normandy. Although he and his staff carefully created messages that were delivered in speeches, press conferences, and letters in the weeks preceding his trip to Germany, he was not able to silence his critics.

Revisiting the Controversy

The controversy surrounding Reagan's trip to West Germany and his response to his critics illustrate the many sides of this complicated individual and highlight his strengths and weaknesses as a leader. Reagan's acceptance of the invitation by Chancellor Helmut Kohl of West Germany to visit a World War II cemetery without considering possible negative implications may be seen as an example of Reagan's lack of interest in seeking information, but it also illustrates his loyalty to a crucial friend and ally. Observers stated that Reagan was extremely loyal to friends. He wanted to repay Kohl for providing military support to the United States in its opposition to the Soviet Union and to make it clear that he could be counted on to support Kohl in any conflict with totalitarian regimes.

Reagan's lack of supervision and the ineffective staff work in his second administration dramatically compounded his problems. Once the conflict surfaced, Reagan's stubbornness became apparent when he refused to change his itinerary even though he found himself in a situation that was damaging his image and his presidency. In the end, he compromised and altered the schedule for the trip by adding a stop at the site of the concentration camp at Bergen-Belsen. He never accepted responsibility for the controversy surrounding the trip, and he attempted unsuccessfully to redefine the situation by arguing that there had been a misunderstanding concerning the original invitation from the West German government. Even if Reagan's speeches and press conferences leading up to the German visit were apologies,[1] in the end he did not effectively apologize and many of his opponents did not accept his efforts to address their concerns. If Reagan speechwriter Josh Gilder's assertions are correct, Reagan may have been less concerned with apologizing and limiting damage with his audiences in the United States than he was in assuring Chancellor Kohl and other European leaders of his support in their opposition to the Soviet Union.[2]

CHAPTER 5

Responding to the Controversy

In situations as complicated as that surrounding Reagan's 1985 trip to Germany, it is possible that there was little potential for public discourse to make a difference. But Reagan had been successful in difficult situations in the past, and he turned to the area of his greatest strength, the power of speech, in an attempt to calm his adversaries and rescue his presidential image. His speechwriters prepared two well-written and well-argued speeches that he felt would improve his image and calm his adversaries. The speeches built on one another and contained many of the same themes and ideas. The speech at Bergen-Belsen focused more on the issue of the Holocaust and the horrible crimes committed by the Nazis during World War II. The Bitburg speech contained many of the same themes, but it was more of a cold war speech in which Reagan told the world that it was time to move from the past to the present. The world should remember the crimes of World War II, but there should be more focus on challenging current tyrants, especially the Soviet Union. In the end, both speeches offered hope for a better world in the future. Both speeches also contained many of the arguments Reagan had used in press conferences, speeches, and letters to the public in the weeks before his trip.

Reagan forced himself to enter a highly emotional setting by visiting the memorial at the site of the Bergen-Belsen concentration camp even though he had a history of not doing well in similar situations. After completing that difficult speech, he moved to a more congenial location among his supporters at the military base at Bitburg. But the potential of success with his speeches was weakened by an inability or unwillingness to change his message—again a sign of his stubbornness. He continued to proclaim a historical interpretation of the events of World War II that offended his opponents, and he either did not understand, or refused to understand, the symbol of the president of the United States honoring German soldiers who had committed some of the worst atrocities of World War II.

The speeches at Bergen-Belsen and Bitburg also illustrate the importance of having a thorough understanding of the audience and the expectations of members of that audience in ceremonial situations. Reagan had been a master at speaking in ceremonial settings through-out his career. He seemed to have an innate sense of what an audience and an event expected or demanded. He had a history of being in touch with audiences in the United States, but he had a lingering doubt about such speeches during international trips. Reagan's weakness in this area may have been summarized well by Richard Reeves: "Words spoken by the leader of the strongest nation in the world were of a different order than were the campaign speeches of an old actor or a right-wing governor."[3] The tremendous success of speeches at Normandy and Omaha Beach in 1984 were vivid examples of how Reagan could speak effectively in ceremonial situations in Europe, but he was not able to sustain his success in Germany the following year. Reagan and his staff seemed to misread the situation and were unable, or unwilling, to make the changes needed in his messages to appeal to important segments of his audience.

The dramatic confrontation leading to May 5, 1985, caused many critics to question Reagan's sensitivity to the needs of Jewish people and his ability to thoroughly understand the significance of the Holocaust, even though he had a long history of supporting Jewish causes and rejecting the horror of the Holocaust. In the minds of many critics, "Bitburg" had become synonymous with Reagan's insensitivity to the feelings of Nazi victims, especially Jews.[4] His carefully crafted speeches could not overcome that feeling among many of his opponents.

On May 6, 1985, Bernard Weinraub wrote this about the German visit: "White House Aides have acknowledged that the Bitburg visit is probably the biggest fiasco of Mr. Reagan's presidency."[5] Lou Cannon's description of the day agrees with Weinraub's: "Bitburg was the semi-nal symbolic disaster of an administration that placed great store on symbolism. In laying a wreath at a German military cemetery that contained the graves of Waffen SS troops, Reagan abandoned the moral high ground of his intense convictions about the Holocaust to satisfy his political relationship with West German Chancellor Helmut Kohl." Cannon continues by describing the failure of the president's staff, par-ticularly the White House chief of staff: "Bitburg exposed the weakness of Don Regan's premise that the Reagan presidency functioned best if Reagan were left to his own devices. It also provided a test of Regan's damage-control abilities, which he badly flunked."[6]

Cannon provides a summary of the negative effects the conflict: "The Bitburg controversy nevertheless left scars that did not heal. Reagan would never again fully recapture the moral high ground he had sacrificed at Bitburg. Even after the events had become a distant memory, he did not regain the trust within the Jewish community that he had taken for granted in the early years of his political career and the first four years of his presidency. Nor was Reagan the only one to bear the scars. Deaver's reputation as master orchestrator was deeply tarnished, and Don Regan had shown himself lacking in the skills of political damage control that had distinguished his predecessor."[7]

Raul Hilburg echoes Cannon's words: "Caught in the middle of a situation his staff had not prepared him for, he confronted a dilemma from which he could not extricate himself. He went with anguish and possible doubts, losing his surefootedness and sacrificing his image as a man who acted out of conviction."[8]

Analyzing the Speeches

Although they often criticized Reagan, Bob Schieffer and Gary Paul Gates do not see the entire Bitburg affair as a failure. They propose that Reagan was able to lessen the damage to his presidency with an effective speech at Bergen-Belsen, but they see the weaknesses apparent during the trip to Germany as a preview of future problems for the Reagan presidency: "The speech that Reagan finally delivered at Bergen-Belsen was one of the most moving of his presidency.... The speech took some of the edge off the controversy, and the entire episode was eventually overtaken by other events. But the Bitburg mess would be remembered as the first major blunder of the post-Baker White House. It set the tone for the far more serious fiascos in foreign policy that cast a pall over the second term of Ronald Reagan's presidency."[9]

Edmund Morris is less generous in his analysis of the speech at Bergen-Belsen: "As literature, Ronald Reagan's Bergen-Belsen eulogy fell short of the *Challenger* tribute and his final telecast as President. As oratory, it did not compare with the eloquence of Charles de Gaulle returning to Paris, or Cardinal Wojtyla revisiting Auschwitz as Pope. Even Elie Wiesel's simple statement in the Roosevelt Room outclassed it. The essential difference, the curse of American good fortune, was that what he merely felt, they actually knew."[10]

Kathryn M. Olson argues that Reagan's speech at Bitburg Air Base was not successful in achieving his goals: "Reagan's symbolic actions preceding and during the trip show how Reagan defined, then attempted to redefine the meaning of the Bitburg visit to make it more palatable to the public. Reagan's failure to satisfy those who accepted the Jewish opposition's position with his definitions and redefinitions of the situation resulted from the fact that he and his opponents proceeded from irreconcilable perspectives."[11] If Olson is correct, the speech Reagan should have delivered at Bitburg would have been significantly different from the one presented. Reagan simply would not consider making the changes Olson thinks were necessary in the situation.

Friedenberg disagrees with Olson's assessment. He seems to say that Reagan was once again able to achieve success in a very difficult situation. His success was the result of his ability to excel in presidential speaking: "Reagan's speech at the Bitburg Air Base was a potent apologia, far stronger than his previous efforts. Doubtlessly, part of the reason was the rhetorical situation. In his prior apologies, situational constraints inherent in press conferences and speeches of presentation limited him; moreover, by responding extemporaneously in the press conference, he made a serious error when he likened German soldiers to the victims of concentration camps. At the Bitburg Air Base, Reagan prepared thoroughly in advance and spoke with virtually no other purpose than to justify his action. . . . Reagan's use of language, which included frequent repetition and parallelism, also lifted this speech to a more eloquent level than his earlier efforts."[12]

Rhetorical critic Jay Plum agrees with Friedenberg, arguing that Reagan's speech at Bitburg was appropriate for the situation and occasion. Reagan's success, according to Plum, illustrates that the nickname "Great Communicator" is truly fitting.[13]

Friedenberg quotes Elie Wiesel about the lasting impact of the trip to Germany and Reagan's speeches: "In the long run . . . the wounds will heal. After all, he is the President and we must deal with his policies, with his staff, with his administration. But the wounds are there and the wounds are deep." Friedenberg points to a *New York Times*–CBS poll conducted the day after the visit. In that poll, 41 percent of the people supported Reagan's actions, 41 percent opposed them, and 18 percent had no opinion. The poll indicated that the Bitburg visit "did not effect President Reagan's overall standing with the public" and that the visit to Bergen-Belsen "diminished the public opposition to the Bitburg visit."[14] The mixed results of the poll seem to reflect the mixed reactions of the critics.

The president and his supporters tried to paint the events of the day in the most positive manner they could. Staffer Michael Deaver said that Reagan's performance had given them all hope that the administration would be viewed in a more positive light: "For all of the grim images and the raw, sobering emotional scars, most of us left Germany in a lighter mood than when we came. The president had endured, had in my mind *overcome* barriers that some feared, or hoped, would endanger his authority." Deaver continues by admitting that the president was not entirely successful in overcoming the concerns of his critics, but he had not given in to the situation of the pessimism of others: "And now it was a time to cleanse the old wounds, the old hatreds. That may have been too idealistic a goal. But that was Reagan. And he pulled us out of a ditch to nearly bring it off. We may still find that he did. At the least, he had taken an explosive and emotional situation and met it with skill and honesty." In the end, Deaver tries to put a positive spin on the day: "The historians will tell us whether the president changed any minds or hearts, or whether the visit to Bitburg damaged his reputation and dishonored the memory of those who fought and died forty years earlier. My instinct tells me that Bitburg will be remembered for a gesture well meant and, against deep-rooted resistance, well timed."[15] Reeves argues that the speech at the cemetery was "anticlimactic, which was the way Deaver had planned it."[16]

Gilder was under tremendous pressure to write the message Reagan delivered at Bitburg. He agrees with Deaver in assessing the trip a success. He feels that Reagan went to West Germany to deliver a strong message to the Soviet Union that the United States and West Germany were strongly united in their opposition to the communists and their followers. The message was clearly and forcefully sent. Because the message was so clear, Gilder believes that the speech "took the wind" out of Reagan's opponents' sails. The opponents either became silent or toned down their criticism. He feels that many of them came to understand Reagan's reason for going to Europe and the importance of the message. In the end, Gilder was thrilled with the speech because he felt that it accomplished far more that he could ever hope.[17]

Events Following the Speeches

Reagan's reaction to the events of the day reflected his innate optimism. Morris describes the conclusion of Reagan's day as the president was being entertained at a castle outside Bonn: "Handsome and happy in white tie and tails, he mounted the marble staircase with his wife at his side. She too wore white, glittering on white. 'Mr. President, how do you assess the day's events sir?' Reagan considered the question. 'It's been a wonderful day!' He strode on into a radiant banqueting hall illuminated by thousands of ivory candles and decorated with green 'trees' of spring flowers. Before he and his host rose to speak, the castle rang with trumpets."[18] If Reagan had any doubts about the events, he certainly did not show them at the reception. He had survived a grueling, difficult day and perhaps felt that it was time to move on to other issues.

In his toast that evening, Reagan describes the events of the day.[19] He continues with many of the themes he used in his speeches earlier, especially his interpretation of history that many Germans were also victims of Hitler: "Today was especially moving. We cannot fully understand the long road we've all traveled since 1945 unless we remember the beginnings. By standing before the mass graves at a spot such as Bergen-Belsen, we could begin—but only begin—to feel the suffering of so many innocent people and to sense the horror which confronted our leaders 40 years ago. And by joining Chancellor Kohl in Bitburg, we could better understand the price paid by the German people for the crimes of the Third Reich." He then reiterates the statement he had used so many times to appeal to Jewish survivors of the Holocaust: "Today, as 40 years ago, the thought uppermost in our minds must remain: Never again."

He describes the progress of democracy in West Germany, the growth of friendship between the United States and Germany since World War II, the problems of dealing with the Soviet Union militarily, the successes of NATO, and the marvelous potential for the future. He concludes with his optimistic belief that the future will be better than the past or the present: "These are not dreams. I believe from the bottom of my heart we have every reason for confidence. The future is on the side of the free. The Federal Republic and the United States have proven that. Our 40 years of friendship are reason enough to rejoice, but let us look to the next 40 years, to the freedom and peace our children and their children will enjoy, to the boundless progress they will make, and to the friendship between Germany and the United States, which will serve them well just as it has served us."

On May 6, Reagan spoke to the citizens of Hambach, Germany.[20] He continues to describe the economic and political growth of Europe since the end of World War II: "Today, only 40 years after the most devastating war known to man, Western Europe has risen in glory from its ruins.... No country in the world has been more creative than Germany, and no other can better help create our future. We have seen one miracle.... The experts expected it would be decades before Germany's economy regained its prewar level. You did it in less than one. The experts said the Federal Republic could not absorb millions of refugees, establish a democracy on the ashes of Nazism, and be reconciled with your neighbors. You did all three."

On his return to the United States on May 10, Reagan spoke of European friendship for the United States and that they know "the United States is working hard for freedom, democracy, and peace, and believe me they appreciate our efforts. I know that you've heard that because there were a few demonstrations, some things might have been going wrong. But you know every time I noticed who was demonstrating, I felt reassured that we were saying and doing the right things."[21] This is an interesting comment because Reagan was never really close to the protesters. In fact, many of the protesters were his Jewish critics, so this comment may have reinforced their feeling that he did not care about them or the Holocaust.

The Bitburg controversy continued to haunt Reagan. On June 18 he participated in a lengthy news conference[22] that dealt with a series of emotional issues such as the highjacking of TWA Flight 847 in Athens and the death of a U.S. serviceman on the flight,[23] the ongoing captivity of other hostages in the Middle East, the public image that Americans were targets for terrorism in the Middle East, and the defeat of important proposals in Congress. At the conclusion of the press conference Reagan was asked if, because of his defeats in Congress, the hostage crisis, and the Bitburg controversy, "the Teflon that's covered your Presidency has slipped off? Is your luck running out?"

Reagan's response is a lengthy one, beginning with the fact that he never had "Teflon on me anyplace." He turns to Bitburg: "And with regard to Bitburg, in spite of the efforts of some of you, from the very first, I felt it was the morally right thing to do. And I'm pleased that I did it. And it was a worthwhile experience over there. And I began to get my reward when I spoke to 10,000 young teenage Germans and at the end heard 10,000 young Germans sing our national anthem in our language. I think it was a recognition." He then returns to several of the themes he repeated throughout the controversy: "Those that indicated that in some way I might be suggesting that we forget the Holocaust—no, in no way. Nor are the Germans trying to forget the Holocaust. I was amazed—in this 40 years now of friendship that has followed all of that hatred and the evil of the Holocaust and of Nazism—to learn that the Germans, not only have they preserved the horrible camps and maintained museums with the photos all blown up of the worst and most despicable things that happened there, but they bring their schoolchildren every year and show them and say that this must never happen again."

He concludes: "I have never suggested in going there that this was a forgive-and-forget thing. It's up to someone else to forgive—not us—if there is any forgiveness, and certainly we must never forget. And so, if there is any Teflon, I didn't think that I lost any on doing that."

Reagan never believed that the trip to Germany was a mistake. On March 10, 1988, a few months before he left office, he was interviewed by Dieter Kronzucker of ZDF Television of Germany.[24] Reagan was asked if he regretted his visit to Bitburg. His answer is consistent with what he had said in 1985: "Not at all. I thought it was very worthwhile, and I came home with a message also for our own people: that I think the courage of your country in maintaining those evidences of the horror of the Holocaust and bringing your own young people to see them so that this can never happen again—I think is something that you have every reason to be proud of."

The events of April and May 1985 say a great deal about Reagan and his reliance on the power of public speaking. When he was truly pressed, Reagan seemed to have a natural inclination to try save his reputation with the spoken word. He had made his reputation as a spokesman for the film industry, as a representative for General Electric, as a campaigner for other politicians, and eventually as governor of California and president of the United States. Even those who disagreed with Reagan's actions and beliefs saw him as a model of presidential oratory, much like his early hero, Franklin D. Roosevelt. In the end, much of what members of the American public remember about Reagan will be based on his speaking in public.

Reagan and his speeches continue to be worthy of study by those who are interested in learning how to construct and deliver a speech. His speeches at Normandy, Bergen-Belsen, and Bitburg are excellent examples of well-researched, well-organized, well-written, and well-delivered ceremonial speeches. The language in the speeches is powerful and evocative of the situation in which they were delivered. The fact that the speeches in Germany were not as successful as he had hoped in no ways lessens their value as models for future speakers, including future presidents of the United States.

Ronald Reagan's Remarks at a Joint German-American Ceremony at Bitburg Air Base in the Federal Republic of Germany May 5, 1985

Thank you very much. I have just come from the cemetery where German war dead lay at rest. No one could visit there without deep and conflicting emotions. I felt great sadness that history could be filled with such waste, destruction, and evil but my heart was also lifted by the knowledge that from the ashes has come hope and that from the terrors of the past we have built 40 years of peace, freedom, and reconciliation among our nations.

This visit has stirred many emotions in the American and German people, too. I've received many letters since first deciding to come to Bitburg cemetery; some supportive, others deeply concerned and questioning, and others opposed. Some old wounds have been reopened, and this I regret very much because this should be a time of healing.

To the veterans and families of American servicemen who still carry the scars and feel the painful losses of that war, our gesture of reconciliation with the German people today in no way minimizes our love and honor for those who fought and died for our country. They gave their lives to rescue freedom in its darkest hour. The alliance of democratic nations that guards the freedom of millions in Europe and America today stands as living testimony that their noble sacrifice was not in vain.

No, their sacrifice was not in vain. I have to tell you that nothing will ever fill me with greater hope than the sight of two former war heroes who met today at the Bitburg ceremony; each among the bravest of the brave; each an enemy of the other 40 years ago; each a witness to the horrors of war. But today they came together, American and German, General Matthew B. Ridgway and General Johannes Steinhoff, reconciled and united for freedom. They reached over the graves to one another like brothers and grasped their hands in peace.

To the survivors of the Holocaust: Your terrible suffering has made you ever vigilant against evil. Many of you are worried that reconciliation means forgetting. Well, I promise you, we will never forget. I have just come this morning from Bergen-Belsen, where the horror of that terrible crime, the Holocaust, was forever burned upon my memory. No, we will never forget, and we say with the victims of that Holocaust: Never again.

The war against one man's totalitarian dictatorship was not like other wars. The evil war of Nazism turned all values upside down. Nevertheless, we can mourn the German war dead today as human beings crushed by a vicious ideology.

There are over 2,000 buried in Bitburg cemetery. Among them are 48 members of the SS—the crimes of the SS must rank among the most heinous in human history—but others buried there were simply soldiers in the German Army. How many were fanatical followers of a dictator and willfully carried out his cruel orders? And how many were conscripts, forced into service during the death throes of the Nazi war machine. We do not know. Many, however, we know from the dates on their tombstones, were only teenagers at the time. There is one boy buried there who died a week before his 16th birthday.

There were thousands of such soldiers to whom Nazism meant no more than a brutal end to a short life. We do not believe in collective guilt. Only God can look into the human heart, and all these men have now met their supreme judge, and they have been judged by Him as we shall all be judged.

Our duty today is to mourn the wreckage of totalitarianism, and today in Bitburg cemetery we commemorated the good in humanity that was consumed back then, 40 years ago. Perhaps if that 15-year-old soldier had lived, he would have joined his fellow countrymen in building this new democratic Federal Republic of Germany, devoted to human dignity and the defense of freedom that we celebrate today. Or perhaps his children or his grandchildren might be among you here today at Bitburg Air Base, where new generations of Germans and Americans join together in friendship and common cause, dedicating their lives to preserving peace and guarding the security of the free world.

Too often in the past each war only planted the seeds of the next. We celebrate today the reconciliation between our two nations that has liberated us from that cycle of destruction. Look at what together we've accomplished. We who were enemies are now friends; we who were bitter adversaries are now the strongest of allies.

In the place of fear we've sown trust, and out of the ruins of war has blossomed an enduring peace. Tens of thousands of Americans have served in this town over the years. As the mayor of Bitburg has said, in that time there have been some 6,000 marriages between Germans and Americans, and many thousands of children have come from these unions. This is the real symbol of our future together, a future to be filled with hope, friendship, and freedom.

The hope that we see now could sometimes be glimpsed in the darkest days of the war. I'm thinking of one special story—that of a mother and her son living alone in a modest cottage in the middle of the woods. And one night as the Battle of the Bulge exploded not far away, and around them, three young American soldiers arrived at their door—they were standing there in the snow, lost behind enemy lines. All were frostbitten; one was badly wounded. Even though sheltering the enemy was punishable by death, she took them in and made them a supper with some of her last food. Then she heard another knock at the door. And this time four German soldiers stood there. The woman was afraid, but she quickly said with a firm voice, "There will be no shooting here." She made all the soldiers lay down their weapons, and they all joined in the makeshift meal. Heinz and Willi, it turned out were only 16; the corporal was the oldest at 23. Their natural suspicion dissolved in the warmth and comfort of the cottage. One of the Germans, a former medical student, tended the wounded American. But now, listen to the rest of the story through the eyes of one who was there, now a grown man, but that young lad had been her son. He said, "The Mother said grace. I noticed that there were tears in her eyes as she said the old, familiar words, 'Komm, Herr Jesus. Be our guest.' And as I looked around the table, I saw tears too, in the eyes of the battle-weary soldiers, boys again, some from America, some from German, all far from home."

That night—as the storm of war tossed the world—they had their own private armistice. And the next morning, the German corporal showed the Americans how to get back behind their own lines. And they all shook hands and went their separate ways. That happened to be Christmas Day, 40 years ago.

Those boys reconciled briefly in the midst of war. Surely we allies in peacetime should honor the reconciliation of the last 40 years.

To the people of Bitburg, our hosts and the hosts of our servicemen, like that generous woman 40 years ago, you make us feel very welcome. Vielen dank. [Many thanks.]

And to the men and women of Bitburg Air Base, I just want to say that we know that even with such wonderful hosts, your job is not an easy one. You serve around the clock far from home, always ready to defend freedom. We're grateful, and we're proud of you.

Four decades ago we waged a great war to lift the darkness of evil from the world, to let men and women in this country and in every country live in the sunshine of liberty. Our victory was great and the Federal Republic, Italy, and Japan are now in the community of free nations. But the struggle for freedom is not complete, for today much of the world is still cast it totalitarian darkness.

Twenty-two years ago President John F. Kennedy went to the Berlin Wall and proclaimed that he, too, was a Berliner. Well, today freedom-loving people around the world must say; I am a Berliner. I am a Jew in a world still threatened by anti-Semitism. I am an Afghan, and I am a prisoner of the Gulag. I am a refugee in a crowded boat floundering off the coast of Vietnam. I am a Laotian, a Cambodian, a Cuban, and a Miskito Indian in Nicaragua. I, too, am a potential victim of totalitarianism.

One lesson of World War II, the one lesson of Nazism, is that freedom must always be stronger than totalitarianism and that good must always be stronger than evil. The moral measure of our two nations will be found in the resolve we show to preserve liberty, to protect life, and to honor and cherish all God's children.

That is why the free, democratic Federal Republic of Germany is such a profound and hopeful testament to the human spirit. We cannot undo the crimes and wars of yesterday nor call back the millions to life, but we can give meaning to the past by learning its lessons and making a better future. We can let our pain drive us to greater efforts to heal humanity's suffering.

Today I've traveled 220 miles from Bergen-Belsen, and I feel, 40 years in time. With the lessons of the past firmly in our minds, we've turned a new, brighter page in history.

One of the many who wrote me about this visit was a young woman who had recently been bas mitzvahed. She urged me to lay the wreath at Bitburg cemetery in honor of the future of Germany. And that is what we've done.

On this 40th anniversary of World War II, we mark the day when the hate, the evil, and the obscenities ended, and we commemorate the rekindling of the democratic spirit in Germany.

There's much to make us hopeful on this historic anniversary. One of the symbols of that hate—that could have been that hope, a little while ago, when we heard a German band playing the American National Anthem and an American band playing the German National Anthem. While much of the world still huddles in the darkness of oppression, we can see a new dawn of freedom sweeping the globe. And we can see in the new democracies of Latin America, in the new economic freedoms and prosperity in Asia, in the slow movement toward peace in the Middle

East, and in the strengthening alliance of democratic nations in Europe and America that the light from that dawn is growing stronger.

Together, let us gather in that light and walk out of the shadow. Let us live in peace.

Thank you, and God bless you all.

Notes

Preface

1. Richard Reeves, *President Reagan: The Triumph of Imagination* (New York: Simon and Schuster, 2005), 7.

Chapter 1

1. Quoted in Ian Jackman, ed., *Ronald Reagan Remembered: CBS News,* (New York: Simon and Schuster, 2004), 116–17. The article originally appeared in *Newsweek,* June 14, 2004.
2. Lou Cannon, *President Reagan: The Role of a Lifetime* (New York: Public Affairs, 2000), ix.
3. Ibid., x.
4. William F. Lewis, "Telling America's Story: Narrative Form and the Reagan Presidency," *Quarterly Journal of Speech* 73 (1987): 280. "Malaise" is an important word in this quote because it was attributed to Reagan's predecessor, Jimmy Carter.
5. Peggy Noonan, *What I Saw at the Revolution* (New York: Random House, 1990), 151.
6. Sarah Russell Hankins, "Archetypal Alloy: Reagan's Rhetorical Image," *Central States Speech Journal* 34 (1983): 33–36.
7. Lewis, "Telling America's Story," 280. The quote is from journalist Mary McGrory.
8. Jane Mayer and Doyle McManus, *Landslide: The Unmaking of the President* (Boston: Houghton Mifflin, 1988), 9–10.
9. Ibid., 10–11.
10. Richard Reeves, *President Reagan: The Triumph of Imagination* (New York: Simon and Schuster, 2005), 8.
11. Thomas L. Friedman, "Thou Shall Not Destroy the Center,"

New York Times, November 11, 2005. http://select.nytimes
.com/2005/11/11/opinion/11friedman.html (accessed November
11, 2005).

12. For more information on genre studies, see Kathleen Hall Jamieson,
"Generic Constraints and the Rhetorical Situation," *Philosophy
and Rhetoric* 6 (1973): 162–79; and Kathleen Hall Jamieson and
Karlyn Kohrs Campbell, "Rhetorical Hybrids: Fusion of Generic
Elements," *Quarterly Journal of Speech* 68 (1982): 146–57.

13. Lewis, "Telling America's Story," 280.

14. Bob Schieffer and Gary Paul Gates, *The Acting President* (New York:
E. F. Dutton, 1989), 23–24.

15. Mayer and McManus, *Landslide,* 21.

16. Ibid., 51.

17. Lewis, "Telling America's Story," 281.

18. Mayer and McManus, *Landslide,* 13.

19. Books that are highly favorable of Reagan include Martin Anderson: *Revolution: The Reagan Legacy* (Stanford, Calif.: Hoover
Institute Press, 1990).

20. For example, Peter Robinson, *How Ronald Reagan Changed My
Life* (New York: ReganBooks, 2003).

21. Anderson, *Revolution,* xxiv.

22. Ibid., xxvi.

23. Ibid., 279.

24. Personal interview with Josh Gilder, December 12, 2005.

25. Anderson, *Revolution,* 290.

26. Lou Cannon, quoted in Jackman, *Ronald Reagan Remembered,*
xiii.

27. Michael Deaver, *Behind the Scenes* (New York: William Morrow,
1987), 73.

28. Ibid., 36.

29. Ibid., 41.

30. Cannon, *President Reagan,* 18.

31. Dan Rather quoted in Jackman, *Ronald Reagan Remembered,*
xi–xii.

32. Deaver, *Behind the Scenes,* 76–77.

33. Kurt Ritter and David Henry, *Ronald Reagan: The Great Communicator* (New York: Greenwood, 1992), 118.

34. Ibid., 118.

35. For an excellent discussion of "The Speech," see Kurt W. Ritter, "Ronald Reagan and 'The Speech': The Rhetoric of Public Relations Politics," *Western Speech* 32 (1968): 50–58.

36. Michael Deaver, *A Different Drummer* (New York: HarperCollins, 2001), 18.

37. Ibid., 165.

38. Personal interview with Josh Gilder.

39. Deaver, *Different Drummer,* 175.

40. Ibid., 54, 56.

41. Ritter and Henry, *Ronald Reagan,* 3–5.

42. Ronald Reagan, *An American Life* (New York: Simon and Schuster, 1990), 247.

43. Garry Wills, *Reagan's America* (New York: Penguin Books, 2000), ix.

44. Noonan, *What I Saw,* 149.

45. David Gergen, *Eyewitness to Power* (New York: Simon and Schuster, 2000), 153.

46. Cannon, *President Reagan,* 18.

47. Robinson, *How Ronald Reagan Changed My Life,* 146.

48. Wills, *Reagan's America,* 394.

49. Mayer and McManus, *Landslide,* 25.

50. Quoted in ibid., 165.

51. Reagan, *American Life,* 161.

52. Anderson, *Revolution,* 57.

53. Ibid., 281.

54. Kathryn M. Olson, "The Controversy over President Reagan's Visit to Bitburg: Strategies of Definition and Redefinition," *Quarterly Journal of Speech* 75 (1989): 129–30. At this point in history, Germany was divided into a democratic West Germany and communist East Germany. The two countries united after the fall of the Berlin Wall in 1989 during the administration of Reagan's successor, George H. W. Bush.

55. Douglas Brinkley, *The Boys of Pointe Du Hoc* (New York: William Morrow, 2005), 200.

56. Personal interview with Josh Gilder.

57. Edmund Morris, *Dutch* (New York: Random House, 1999), 514.

58. "Address to the Nation on the Explosion of the Space Shuttle Challenger January 28, 1986." *The Public Papers of President Ronald W. Reagan.* Ronald Reagan Presidential Library, http://www.reagan .utexas.edu/archives/speeches/1986/12886b.htm (accessed November 29, 2005). For a thorough analysis of that speech, see Mary E. Stuckey, *Slipping the Surly Bonds: Reagan's Challenger Address* (College Station: Texas A&M University Press, 2006).

59. "Remarks on East-West Relations at the Brandenburg Gate in West Berlin June 12, 1987." *The Public Papers of President Ronald W. Reagan.* Ronald Reagan Presidential Library, http://www .reagan.utexas.edu/archives/speeches/1987/061287d.htm (accessed November 29, 2005).

60. Ken Duberstein, quoted in Brinkley, *Boys of Pointe Du Hoc,* 6. For a text of the *Challenger* disaster speech, see Ritter and Henry, *Ronald Reagan,* 173–75, and Lloyd Rohler and Roger Cook, eds., *Great Speeches for Criticism and Analysis,* 2d ed. (Greenwood, Ind.: Alistair, 1993), 314–15.

61. Brinkley, *Boys of Pointe Du Hoc,* 3, 5, 9.

62. Ken Duberstein, quoted in ibid., 5.

63. Ibid., 6–7.

64. Lou Cannon, quoted in ibid., 7.

65. Hugh Heclo, quoted in ibid., 106.

66. Ibid., 200.

67. Cannon, *President Reagan,* 507.

68. Ibid., 507.

69. Reagan, *American Life,* 27.

70. Noonan, *What I Saw,* 150.

71. Quoted in ibid., 153.

72. Reagan, *American Life,* 31.

73. Ibid., 33.

74. Noonan, *What I Saw,* 153–54.

75. Reagan, *American Life,* 28.
76. Wills, *Reagan's America,* 36–37.
77. Quoted in Ritter and Henry, *Ronald Reagan,* 5.
78. Wills, *Reagan's America,* 128–29
79. Quoted in Ritter and Henry, *Ronald Reagan,* 5. The quote originally appeared in the *Dixon [Illinois] Evening Telegraph,* September 13, 1941, 2:17.
80. Wills, *Reagan's America,* 135–36.
81. Ritter and Henry, *Ronald Reagan,* 6.
82. Ibid., 6.
83. Ibid., 6.
84. Ibid., 11–12.
85. Ibid., 15.
86. Deaver, *A Different Drummer,* 1.
87. Cannon, *President Reagan,* 10–11.
88. Reagan, *American Life,* 28.
89. Wills, *Reagan's America,* x.
90. Paul Erickson, *Reagan Speaks: The Making of an American Myth* (New York: New York University Press, 1985), 2, 7, 16, 51, 61.
91. Robinson, *How Ronald Reagan Changed My Life,* 132.
92. Cannon, *President Reagan,* 95.
93. Ibid., 96–97.
94. Noonan, *What I Saw,* xiii.
95. Ibid., 158.
96. Gergen, *Eyewitness to Power,* 152, 247.
97. Reagan, *American Life,* 393, 42.
98. Tony Dolan, quoted in Robinson, *How Ronald Reagan Changed My Life,* 69–71.

Chapter 2

1. Celeste Michelle Condit, "The Functions of Epideictic: The Boston Massacre Orations as Exemplar," *Communication Quarterly* 33 (Fall 1985): 285.
2. Waldo W. Braden and Harold Mixon, "Epideictic Speaking in the

Post–Civil War South and the Southern Experience," *Southern Communication Journal* 54 (Fall 1988): 44.

3. Ibid.

4. Bonnie J. Dow, "The Function of Epideictic and Deliberative Strategies in Presidential Crisis Rhetoric," *Western Journal of Speech Communication* 53 (Summer 1989): 296–300.

5. Braden and Mixon, "Epideictic Speaking," 54.

6. Mary E. Stuckey, *Slipping the Surly Bonds: Reagan's* Challenger *Address* (College Station: Texas A&M University Press, 2006), 10.

7. Condit, "Functions of Epideictic," 288.

8. Ibid., 289–290.

9. Ibid., 290–91.

10. Ibid., 296–97.

11. Kurt Ritter and David Henry, *Ronald Reagan: The Great Communicator* (New York: Greenwood, 1992), 4–5, 105.

12. Ibid., 8, 93.

13. William F. Lewis, "Telling America's Story: Narrative Form and the Reagan Presidency," *Quarterly Journal of Speech* 73 (1987): 281.

14. Quoted in Richard Reeves, *President Reagan: The Triumph of Imagination* (New York: Simon and Schuster, 2005), 207.

15. Lewis, "Telling America's Story," 281.

16. Ibid., 281–82.

17. Ibid., 282–83.

18. Ibid., 284, 285.

19. Ibid., 289–90.

20. Davis W. Houck and Amos Kiewe, *Actor, Ideologue, Politician: The Public Speeches of Ronald Reagan* (Westport, Conn.: Greenwood, 1993), 1, 331.

21. Ritter and Henry, *Ronald Reagan*, 120.

22. Garry Wills, *Reagan's America* (New York: Penguin Books, 2000), 197.

23. Ibid., 197, 338.

24. John Murphy, "Epideictic and Deliberative Strategies in Opposition to War: The Paradox of Honor and Expediency," *Communication Studies* 43 (Summer 1992): 68.

25. Wills, *Reagan's America*, 379.

26. Lou Cannon, *President Reagan: The Role of a Lifetime* (New York: Public Affairs, 2000), 18.

27. Ibid., xv–xvi, 17–18.

28. Ronald Reagan, quoted in ibid., 21. The quote originally was printed in Ronald Reagan, *Speaking My Mind* (New York: Simon and Schuster, 1989), 14.

29. Cannon, *President Reagan*, 21.

30. Ibid., 21.

31. Ronald Reagan, *An American Life* (New York: Simon and Schuster, 1990), 130.

32. Martin Anderson, *Revolution: The Reagan Legacy* (Stanford, Calif.: Hoover Institute Press, 1990), 49–52.

33. Ken Khachigian, quoted in Ritter and Henry, *Ronald Reagan*, 116.

34. Quoted in ibid., 117.

35. Reagan, *American Life*, 247.

36. Quoted in Ritter and Henry, *Ronald Reagan*, 115.

37. David Gergen, *Eyewitness to Power* (New York: Simon and Schuster, 2000), 212–40.

38. Anderson, *Revolution*, 54.

39. Peter Robinson, *How Ronald Reagan Changed My Life* (New York: ReganBooks, 2003), 151.

40. John Meyer, "Ronald Reagan and Humor: A Politician's Velvet Weapon," *Communication Studies* (Spring 1990): 76–88.

41. Cannon, *President Reagan*, 18.

42. Peggy Noonan, *What I Saw at the Revolution* (New York: Random House, 1990), 4.

43. Ibid., 4.

44. Ibid., 52.

45. Reagan, *American Life*, 246, 247.

46. Robinson, *How Ronald Reagan Changed My Life*, 3.

47. Ibid., 4, 94–95, 9.

48. Ibid., 44–45.

49. Ibid., 105.

50. Personal interview, December 12, 2005.

51. Gergen, *Eyewitness,* 240.

52. Noonan, *What I Saw,* 67.

53. Ibid., 83–84.

54. Reeves, *President Reagan,* 223.

55. This and following quotations from this speech taken from Ronald Reagan, "Remarks at a Ceremony Commemorating the 40th Anniversary of the Normandy Invasion, D-day June 6, 1984," *The Public Papers of President Ronald W. Reagan.* Ronald Reagan Presidential Library, http://www.reagan.utexas.edu/archives/speeches/1984/60684a.htm (accessed November 26, 2005).

56. Noonan, *What I Saw,* 85.

57. This note appears after the text of Reagan's speech in *Public Papers.*

58. Reagan, *American Life,* 374–75.

59. Douglas Brinkley, *The Boys of Point Du Hoc* (New York: William Morrow, 2005), 157, 185.

60. Garry Wills, quoted in ibid., 187.

61. Reagan, *American Life,* 375.

62. This and following quotations from this speech taken from Ronald Reagan, "Remarks at a United States-France Ceremony Commemorating the 40th Anniversary of the Normandy Invasion, D-day June 6, 1984." *The Public Papers of President Ronald W. Reagan.* Ronald Reagan Presidential Library, http://www.reagan.utexas.edu/archives/speeches/1984/60684b.htm (accessed November 26, 2005).

63. Reagan, *American Life,* 376.

64. Michael K. Deaver, *Behind the Scenes* (New York: William Morrow, 1987), 177.

65. Brinkley, *Boys of Point Du Hoc,* 193.

66. Robinson, *How Ronald Reagan Changed My Life,* 112.

Chapter 3

1. Michael Deaver, *A Different Drummer: My Thirty Years with Ronald Reagan* (New York: William Morrow), 103–104.
2. Edmund Morris, *Dutch* (New York: Random House, 1999), 515.
3. Lou Cannon, *President Reagan: The Role of a Lifetime* (New York: Public Affairs, 2000), 509.
4. Elie Wiesel, quoted in Morris, *Dutch*, 521. Ironically, April 11 was the anniversary of the date Wiesel was to have been executed by the Germans in 1945. Fortunately, he was rescued by American soldiers.
5. Kathryn M. Olson, "The Controversy over President Reagan's Visit to Bitburg: Strategies of Definintion and Redefinition," *Quarterly Journal of Speech* 95 (1989): 130.
6. Richard Reeves, *President Reagan: The Triumph of Imagination* (New York: Simon and Schuster, 2005), 249.
7. Quoted in Ed Magnuson, "A Misbegotten Trip Opens New Wounds," *Time*, April 29, 1985, 19. The quote also appears in Jay Plum, "A Rhetorical Analysis of Reagan's Discourse at Bitburg," *North Dakota Journal of Speech and Theatre* (1987), http://www2 .edutech.nodak.edu/ndsta/plum.htm (accessed August 29, 2006).
8. Olson, "Controversy," 129–31.
9. Robert V. Friedenberg, "Elie Wiesel vs. President Ronald Reagan: The Visit to Bitburg," in *Oratorical Encounters*, ed. Halford Ross Ryan (Westport Conn.: Greenwood, 1988), 272–75.
10. Deaver, *Different Drummer*, 104.
11. Ronald Reagan, *An American Life* (New York: Simon and Schuster, 1990), 380.
12. Cannon, *President Reagan*, 510.
13. Reagan, *American Life*, 377. The diary note is from April 4–14.
14. Ibid., 380–81.
15. Garry Wills, *Reagan's America* (New York: Penguin Books, 2000), 201.
16. Michael Deaver, *Behind the Scenes* (New York: William Morrow, 1987), 179.

17. Bob Schieffer and Gary Paul Gates, *The Acting President* (New York: E. P. Dutton, 1989), 205.

18. Deaver, *Behind the Scenes*, 180, 103.

19. Ibid., 184.

20. Reagan, *American Life*, 377. The diary note is from April 15.

21. Details from "Bergen-Belsen," on the website of the United States Holocaust Memorial Museum, Washington, D.C., http://www.ushmm.org/wlc/article.php?lang=en&ModuleId=10005224&printing=yes (accessed July 27, 2006).

22. Quoted in Cannon, *President Reagan*, 511.

23. Quotations and discussion of this conference from "Remarks at a Conference on Religious Liberty, April 16, 1985." *The Public Papers of President Ronald W. Reagan*. Ronald Reagan Presidential Library, http://www.reagan.utexas.edu/archives/speeches/1985/41685d.htm (accessed March 23, 2005).

24. Schieffer and Gates, *Acting President*, 204.

25. Michael Horowitz, quoted in Peggy Noonan, *What I Saw at the Revolution* (New York: Random House, 1990), 213.

26. Quotations and discussion of this meeting from "Remarks and a Question-and-Answer Session with Regional Editors and Broadcasters, April 18, 1985," in *Public Papers of the Presidents of the United States: Ronald Reagan 1985,* Book 1 (Washington, D.C.: Government Printing Office, 1988), 456–57.

27. Quotations and discussion from "Remarks on Presenting the Congressional Gold Medal to Elie Wiesel and on Signing the Jewish Heritage Week Proclamation, April 19, 1985." *The Public Papers of President Ronald W. Reagan*. Ronald Reagan Presidential Library, http://www.reagan.utexas.edu/archives/speeches/1985/41985a.htm (accessed March 23, 2005).

28. Cannon, *President Reagan*, 512.

29. Ibid., 2–4.

30. Morris, *Dutch*, 526.

31. Schieffer and Gates, *Acting President*, 208.

32. Morris, *Dutch*, 526.

33. Reagan, *American Life*, 379. The diary note is from April 19.

34. Cannon, *President Reagan*, 427–29.
35. Morris, *Dutch*, 526.
36. Cannon, *President Reagan*, 430–31.
37. Reagan, *American Life*, 99.
38. Ibid., 99–100.
39. Deaver, *Behind the Scenes*, 177.
40. Cannon, *President Reagan*, 431.
41. Morris, *Dutch*, 527.
42. "Remarks at a Ceremony Honoring Youth Volunteers, April 25, 1985." *The Public Papers of President Ronald W. Reagan*. Ronald Reagan Presidential Library, http://www.reagan.utexas.edu/ar chives/speeches/1985/42585a.htm (accessed March 23, 2005).
43. Quotations and discussion of this meeting from "Interview with Foreign Journalists, April 25, 1985." *The Public Papers of President Ronald W. Reagan*. Ronald Reagan Presidential Library, http://www .reagan.utexas.edu/archives/speeches/1985/42585e.htm (accessed March 23, 2005).
44. Quotations and discussion from "Interview with Foreign Journalists, April 29, 1985." *The Public Papers of President Ronald W. Reagan*. Ronald Reagan Presidential Library, http://www.reagan .utexas.edu/archives/speeches/1985/42985g.htm (accessed March 23, 2005).
45. Quotations and discussion from "Why Going to Bitburg?" folder "Bitburg (3)," box 90417, James M. Rentschler Files, Ronald Reagan Library.
46. "Bitburg (4)," box 90417, James M. Rentschler Files, Ronald Reagan Library.
47. "Memorandum for William Henkel," folder "Bitburg Trip Material, 2 of 3," box OA 17133, Rudy Bessera Files, Ronald Reagan Library.
48. "Memorandum for Ed Rollins," folder "Bitburg Trip Material," box OA 17133, Rudy Besserra Files, Ronald Reagan Library.
49. "Memorandum for Donald Regan," folder "Bitburg Trip Material," box OA 17133, Rudy Besserra Files, Ronald Reagan Library.
50. Breger notes also that there "is a third approach advanced by the Soviets today and by some politicians during and immediately

after World War II—that the Teutonic character is genetically militaristic. We, of course, reject this communal taint."

51. "President's Appearance at Bergen-Belsen," folder "Bitbury Trip Material," Rudy Besserra Files, Ronald Reagan Library.

52. Rudy Besserra Files, Ronald Reagan Library.

53. Deaver, *Behind the Scenes,* 182.

54. "May 5th RR speech," folder "Bergen-Belsen Concentration Camp," box OA 223, Speechwriting: White House Office of Speech Writers Files, Ronald Reagan Library.

55. Cannon, *President Reagan,* 507.

56. Morris, *Dutch,* 528.

57. Ibid., 529.

58. "Meeting w/President Reagan, Oval Office 4–26–85," folder "Bergen-Belsen Concentration Camp," box OA 223, Speechwriting: White House Office of Speech Writers Files, Ronald Reagan Library. There are two versions of these notes. The original in Khachigian's handwriting and a typed version titled "Notes from meeting with P—t, Deaver—Henkel." The notes were quickly typed and full of errors. The two versions are somewhat different, but the typed version seems to be the one used to begin writing the text.

59. "Bergen-Belsen Concentration Camp," Ronald Reagan Library.

60. "Presidential Remarks: Bergen-Belsen Concentration Camp, May 5, 1985," folder "Bergen-Belsen Concentration Camp," box 223, White House Office of Speech Writers Files, Ronald Reagan Library.

61. Ibid.

62. "Presidential Remarks: Bergen-Belsen Concentration Camp," folder "Bergen-Belsen Concentration Camp," box 17, 890, Research Office Records, White House Office of Speech Writers Files, Ronald Reagan Library.

63. "Master, Remarks: Bergen-Belsen Concentration Camp," folder "Bergen-Belsen Concentration Camp," box 223, White House Office of Speech Writers Files, Ronald Reagan Library.

64. "Presidential Remarks: Bergen-Belsen Concentration Camp," folder "Bergen-Belsen Concentration Camp," box 222, White House Office of Speech Writers Files, Ronald Reagan Library.

65. Personal interview, December 12, 2005.
66. "Presential Remarks: Luncheon at Bitburg A.F.B, Bitburg Germany, Sunday, May 5, 1985," box 223, White House Office of Speech Writers Files, Ronald Reagan Library.
67. Personal interview, December 12, 2005.
68. "Presential Remarks: Luncheon at Bitburg A.F.B, Bitburg Germany, Sunday, May 5, 1985," box 223, White House Office of Speech Writers Files, Ronald Reagan Library.
69. "Remarks on Departure for Europe, April 30, 1985," in *Public Papers of the Presidents: Ronald Reagan 1985,* Book 1 (Washington, D.C.: Government Printing Office, 1985), 546–47.
70. "Radio Address to the Nation of the Bonn Economic Summit, May 4, 1985." *The Public Papers of President Ronald W. Reagan.* Ronald Reagan Presidential Library, http://www.reagan.utexas.edu/archives/speeches/1985/50485b.htm (accessed July 18, 2005).

Chapter 4

1. Bernard Weinraub, "Reagan Joins Kohl in Brief Memorial at Bitburg Graves," in Geoffrey Hartman, ed., *Bitburg in Moral and Political Perspective* (Bloomington: Indiana University Press, 1986), 146. The article was originally published in the *New York Times,* May 6, 1985.
2. Lou Cannon, *President Reagan: The Role of a Lifetime* (New York: Public Affairs, 2000), 432.
3. Ibid., 507.
4. Edmund Morris, *Dutch* (New York: Random House, 1999), 529.
5. Weinraub, "Reagan Joins Kohl," 148.
6. Cannon, *President Reagan,* 432.
7. Kohl's speech from "Address by Chancellor Helmut Kohl to President Reagan during the Visit to the Former Concentration Camp at Bergen-Belsen, May 5, 1985," in Hartman, *Bitburg in Moral and Political Perspective,* 252–53.
8. Quotations from "Remarks at a Commemorative Ceremony at Bergen-Belsen Concentration Camp in the Federal Republic of

Germany May 5, 1985." *The Public Papers of President Ronald W. Reagan.* Ronald Reagan Presidential Library, http://www.reagan .utexas.edu/archives/speeches/1985/50585a.htm (accessed July 18, 2005).

9. For Lincoln's first inaugural speech, see Abraham Lincoln, "First Inaugural Address (1861)," in James Andrews and David Zarefsky, eds., *American Voices: Significant Speeches in American History, 1640–1945* (New York: Longman, 1989), 283–91.

10. Weinraub, "Reagan Joins Kohl," 148.

11. Morris, *Dutch,* 529–30.

12. Ibid., 531.

13. Ronald Reagan, *An American Life* (New York: Simon and Schuster, 1990), 382.

14. Quoted in Jason Manning, "The Eighties Club: The Politics and Pop Culture of the 1980." http://eightiesclub.tripod.com/id342.htm (accessed August 30, 2006).

15. Cannon, *President Reagan,* 432–33.

16. John Tagliabue, "The Two Ceremonies at Bergen-Belsen," in Hartman, *Bitburg in Moral and Political Perspective,* 141–43. The article originally appeared in the *New York Times,* May 6, 1985.

17. For a description of the dissent, see James M. Markham, "For Bitburg, Day of Anger Ends Quietly," in ibid., 150–52.

18. Weinraub, "Reagan Joins Kohl," 149

19. Ibid., 146.

20. Richard Reeves, *President Reagan: The Triumph of Imagination* (New York: Simon and Schuster, 2005), 255.

21. Quoted in Hartman, *Bitburg in Moral and Political Perspective,* 176. The editorial appeared in the *Washington Post,* May 6, 1985.

22. Morris, *Dutch,* 532.

23. Cannon, *President Reagan,* 519.

24. Reagan, *American Life,* 383.

25. "Address by Chancellor Helmut Kohl to German and American Soldiers and Their Families at Bitburg, May 5, 1985," in Hartman, *Bitburg in Moral and Political Perspective,* 256–57.

26. Quotations for this speech from "Remarks at a Joint German-

American Military Ceremony at Bitburg Air Base in the Federal Republic of Germany May 5, 1985." *The Public Papers of President Ronald W. Reagan.* Ronald Reagan Presidential Library, http://www.reagan.utexas.edu/archives/speeches/1985/50585b.htm (accessed July 18, 2005).

27. Personal interview December 12, 2005.
28. Ibid.
29. Fritz Vincken, "Truce in the Forest," *Reader's Digest,* January 1973, 111–14. Letter dated October 18, 1965, Bitburg Background, box 17, 890, Research Office Records, White House Office of Speech Writers Files, Ronald Reagan Library.
30. For an excellent discussion of light and dark metaphors, see Michael Osborn, "Archetypal Metaphor in Rhetoric: The Light-Dark Family," *Quarterly Journal of Speech* 53 (1967): 115–16.
31. For Kennedy's comments, see John F. Kennedy, "Ich Bin ein Berliner," in James R. Andrews, *A Choice of Worlds* (New York: Harper and Row, 1973), 79–81.
32. The letter is from Beth Flom, a thirteen-year-old girl from Morganville, New Jersey. The original is in Remarks: Lunch at Bitburg AFB, Bitburg, Germany, box 17, 890, Research Office Records, White Hours Office of Speech Writers, Ronald Reagan Library.
33. Reagan, *American Life,* 383.
34. Ibid., 384.
35. James E. Young, "Memory and Monument," in Hartman, *Bitburg in Moral and Political Perspective,* 103–13.
36. Marouf Hasian Jr., "Anne Frank, Bergen-Belsen, and the Polysemic Nature of Holocaust Memories," *Rhetoric and Public Affairs* 4 (2001): 351.
37. Ibid., 354.
38. Ibid., 355–58.
39. Otto Frank, quoted in ibid., 365.
40. Ibid., 365.
41. Ibid., 367.

Chapter 5

1. Robert V. Friedenberg, "Elie Wiesel vs. President Ronald Reagan," in Halford Ross Ryan, ed., *Oratorical Encounters* (Westport, Conn.: Greenwood, 1988), 267–80.

2. Personal interview with Josh Gilder, December 12, 2005.

3. Richard Reeves, *President Reagan: The Triumph of Imagination* (New York: Simon and Schuster, 2005), 110.

4. Lou Cannon, *President Reagan: The Role of a Lifetime* (New York: Public Affairs, 2000), 431.

5. Bernard Weinraub, "Reagan Joins Kohl in Brief Memorial at Bitburg Graves," in Geoffrey Hartman, ed., *Bitburg in Moral and Political Perspective* (Bloomington: Indiana University Press, 1986), 147. This article originally appeared in the *New York Times*, May 6, 1985.

6. Cannon, *President Reagan*, 506.

7. Ibid., 519.

8. Raul Hilburg, "Bitburg as Symbol," in Hartman, *Bitburg in Moral and Political Perspective*, 25.

9. Bob Schieffer and Gary Paul Gates, *The Acting President* (New York: E. P. Dutton, 1989), 210.

10. Edmund Morris, *Dutch* (New York: Random House, 1999), 531.

11. Kathryn M. Olson, "The Controversy over President Reagan's Visit to Bitburg: Strategies of Definition and Redefinition," *Quarterly Journal of Speech* 75 (1989): 131.

12. Friedenberg, "Elie Wiesel," 275.

13. Jay Plum, "A Rhetorical Analysis of Reagan's Discourse at Bitburg," *North Dakota Journal of Speech and Theatre* (1987), http://www2.edutech.nodak.edu/ndsta/plum.htm (accessed August 29, 2006).

14. Friedenberg, "Elie Wiesel," 275–76.

15. Michael K. Deaver, *Behind the Scenes* (New York: William Morrow, 1987), 188–89.

16. Reeves, *President Reagan*, 255.

17. Personal interview, December 12, 2005.

18. Morris, *Dutch,* 532.
19. "Toast at the State Dinner in Bonn, Federal Republic of Germany, May 5, 1985." *The Public Papers of President Ronald W. Reagan.* Ronald Reagan Presidential Library, http://www.reagan.utexas.edu/archives/speeches/1985/50585c.htm (accessed July 18, 2005).
20. "Remarks to the Citizens in Hambach, Federal Republic of Germany, May 6, 1985." *The Public Papers of President Ronald W. Reagan.* Ronald Reagan Presidential Library, http://www.reagan.utexas.edu/archives/speeches/1985/50685a.htm (accessed August 18, 2005).
21. "Remarks upon Returning from Europe, May 10, 1985," in *Public Papers of the Presidents of the United States: Ronald Reagan 1985,* Book 1 (Washington, D.C.: Government Printing Office, 1988), 602.
22. "The President's News Conference June 18, 1985." *The Public Papers of President Ronald W. Reagan.* Ronald Reagan Presidential Library, http://www.reagan.utexas.edu/archives/speeches/1985/61885c.htm (accessed March 23, 2005).
23. On June 14, 1985, TWA Flight 847 left Athens bound for Rome. There were 135 Americans on the plane. The plane was highjacked by two Arabs who forced the pilot to fly to Beirut, then to Algiers, and then back to Beirut. While the plane was in Beirut the second time, the highjackers beat to death a U.S. Navy diver named Robert Dean Stethem and dumped his body on the tarmac. The plane was refueled and flew to Algiers and then returned to Beirut a third time on June 16. Most of the passengers had been released, but thirty-nine American passengers and crew members were taken hostage and held in Lebanon. The main purpose of the highjacking was to force Israel to release 700 prisoners they had taken during the Israeli invasion of Lebanon. The hostages were released on June 30. Reagan's public approval was helped by his handling of the hostage situation. For a summary of the incident, see Cannon, *President Reagan,* 535–41.

24. "Interview with Dieter Kronzucker of ZDF Television of the Federal Republic of Germany, March 10, 1988." *The Public Papers of President Ronald W. Reagan.* Ronald Reagan Presidential Library, http://www.reagan.utexas.edu/archives/speeches/1988/031088d .htm (accessed March 25, 2005).

Bibliography

Manuscript Sources

Rudy Beserra Files, Ronald W. Reagan Presidential Library, Simi Valley, California.
James Rentschler Files, Ronald W. Reagan Presidential Library, Simi Valley, California.
White House Office of Speech Writers Files, Research Files, Ronald W. Reagan Presidential Library, Simi Valley, California.
White House Office of Speech Writers Files, Speech Drafts, Ronald W. Reagan Presidential Library, Simi Valley, California.

Published Sources

Anderson, Martin. *Revolution: The Reagan Legacy.* Stanford, Calif.: Hoover Institute Press, 1990.
Braden, Waldo W., and Harold Mixon. "Epideictic Speaking in the Post–Civil War South and the Southern Experience." *Southern Communication Journal* 54 (1988): 40–57.
Brinkley, Douglas. *The Boys of Pointe Du Hoc.* New York: William Morrow, 2005.
Cannon, Lou. *President Reagan: The Role of a Lifetime.* New York: Public Affairs, 2000.
Condit, Celeste Michelle. "The Functions of Epideictic: The Boston Massacre Orations as Exemplar." *Communication Quarterly* 33 (1985): 284–99.
Deaver, Michael. *Behind the Scenes.* New York: William Morrow, 1987.
_____. *A Different Drummer: My Thirty Years with Ronald Reagan.* New York: HarperCollins, 2001.

Dow, Bonnie J. "The Function of Epideictic and Deliberative Strategies in Presidential Crisis Rhetoric." *Western Journal of Speech Communication* 53 (1989): 294–310.

Erickson, Paul. *Reagan Speaks: The Making of an American Myth.* New York: New York University Press, 1985.

Friedenberg, Robert V. "Elie Wiesel vs. President Ronald Reagan," in Halford Ross Ryan, ed., *Oratorical Encounters.* Westport, Conn.: Greenwood, 1988.

Gergen, David. *Eyewitness to Power.* New York: Simon and Schuster, 2000.

Hankins, Sarah Russell. "Archetypal Alloy: Reagan's Rhetorical Image." *Central States Speech Journal* 34 (1983): 33–43.

Hartman, Geoffrey H., ed. *Bitburg in Moral and Political Perspective.* Bloomington: Indiana University Press, 1986.

Hasian, Marouf, Jr. "Anne Frank, Bergen-Belsen, and the Polysemic Nature of Holocaust Memories." *Rhetoric and Public Affairs* 4 (2001): 349–74.

Houck, Davis W., and Amos Kiewe. *Actor, Ideologue, Politician: The Public Speeches of Ronald Reagan.* Westport, Conn.: Greenwood Press, 1993.

Jackman, Ian, ed. *Ronald Reagan Remembered: CBS News.* New York: Simon and Schuster, 2004.

Lewis, William F. "Telling America's Story: Narrative Form and the Reagan Presidency." *Quarterly Journal of Speech* 73 (1987): 280–302.

Magnuson, Ed. "A Misbegotten Trip Opens Old Wounds." *Time,* April 29, 1985, 18–23.

Mayer, Jane, and Doyle McManus. *Landslide: The Unmaking of the President.* Boston: Houghton Mifflin, 1988.

Meyer, John. "Ronald Reagan and Humor: A Politician's Velvet Glove." *Communication Studies* 41 (1990): 76–88.

Morris, Edmund. *Dutch.* New York: Random House, 1999.

Murphy, John M. "Epideictic and Deliberative Strategies in Opposition to War: The Paradox of Honor and Expediency." *Communication Studies* 43 (1992): 65–78.

Noonan, Peggy. *What I Saw at the Revolution*. New York: Random House, 1990.

_____. *When Character Was King: A Story of Ronald Reagan*. New York: Viking, 2001.

Olson, Kathryn M. "The Controversy over President Reagan's Visit to Bitburg: Strategies of Definition and Redefinition." *Quarterly Journal of Speech* (1989): 129–51.

Plum, Jay. "A Rhetorical Analysis of Reagan's Discourse at Bitburg." *North Dakota Journal of Speech and Theatre* (1987). http://www2 .edutech.nodak.edu/ndsta/plum.htm.

Public Papers of the Presidents of the United States: Ronald Reagan 1985, Book 1. Washington, D.C.: Government Printing Office, 1988.

Reagan, Ronald. *An American Life*. New York: Simon and Schuster, 1990.

_____. *Speaking My Mind*. New York: Simon and Schuster, 1989.

Reeves, Richard. *President Reagan: The Triumph of Imagination*. New York: Simon and Schuster, 2005.

Ritter, Kurt. "Ronald Reagan and 'The Speech': The Rhetoric of Public Relations Politics." *Western Speech* 32 (1968): 50–58.

Ritter, Kurt, and David Henry. *Ronald Reagan: The Great Communicator*. New York: Greenwood, 1992.

Robinson, Peter. *How Ronald Reagan Changed My Life*. New York: ReganBooks, 2003.

Rohler, Lloyd, and Roger Cook, eds. *Great Speeches for Criticism and Analysis*, 2d ed. Greenwood, Ind.: Alistair, 1993.

Schieffer, Bob, and Gary Paul Gates. *The Acting President*. New York: E. F. Dutton, 1989.

Stuckey, Mary E. *Slipping the Surly Bonds: Reagan's* Challenger *Address*. College Station: Texas A&M University Press, 2006.

Wills, Garry. *Reagan's America*. New York: Penguin Books, 2000.

Index